Miami Beach: Blueprint of an Eden

Lives Seen through the Prism of Family and Place

Michele Oka Doner and Mitchell Wolfson Jr.

Miami Beach: Blueprint of an Eden
Lives Seen through the Prism of Family and Place

FEIERABEND
UNIQUE BOOKS

Previous spread:
A languorous Gertrude
Heller, with Frangipani in
her hair. Newly arrived in
Eden, she enjoys the
shelter of a cluster of palm
fronds, 1938.

Detail from cast plaster
auditorium plaque, Carib
Theatre, 1950. Michael J.
DeAngelis, Architect.
Drawing by M. D. Nimciv.

First Edition
© 2005
Michele Oka Doner and
Mitchell Wolfson Jr.

Introduction © 2005
Alastair Gordon

Published in 2005 by:
Feierabend Unique Books
Judenpfad 61
D-50996 Cologne
Fax +49 2236.337622
fub@artwork-factory.com

ISBN 3-89985-330-x

Printed in Germany

Creative Director:
Jordan Schaps

Art Director:
Peter Feierabend

Layout and Typography:
Rebecca Rose
Stephanie Leifert
Frank Behrendt

Producer:
Lea Nickless

Editors:
Arlene Raven
Suzanne Ramljak
Frederick Doner

Reader:
Kate Daly

Reproduction:
Farbo print+media GmbH
Germany

Contents

Introduction by Alastair Gordon

Michele Oka Doner sits beneath a Caribbean Pigeon tree—one of her favorite trees—and recites "Nomad Exquisite" in a proper schoolgirl cadence. *As the immense dew of Florida / Brings forth / The big-finned palm...* We're having lunch at a restaurant near the beach, sitting beneath the prickly arches of the seventy-year-old tree, leafy shadows across our plates, eating coconut-encrusted shrimp with mango chutney. Like most visitors, I choose the privilege of ignorance when coming to Miami, but even this node of seemingly superficial beach culture has a story that goes deeper than one imagines. To an outsider loaded with northeastern prejudice, it comes as a surprise: first of all that Michele knows Stevens by heart and secondly that this city might possess a poetic soul after all, not just a sequence of facades and false fronts. *And green vine angering for life...* Michele continues, sounding as if she has recited these lines many times. *As the immense dew of Florida / Brings forth hymn and hymn / From the beholder, / Beholding all these green sides / And gold sides of green sides...*

Her Miami Beach begins here, under the shade of this glorious tree and the flamboyant plants of Florida and their gold sides of green sides. It's easy to see how her own art—her castings of pods, roots, fronds and coiling leaves—grows directly from this same source. I had never thought to connect it with Stevens's "immense dew" or the furtive, sloppy eagerness with which everything takes root here: *And blessed mornings, / Meet for the eye of the young alligator, / And lightning colors / So, in me, come flinging / Forms, flames, and the flakes of flames.* These few lines of verse suddenly alter the overall perception of the place and one is able to reconstruct a different version from those same words, switching suddenly from the opening credits of *Miami Vice* to the "angering for life" that drives the vines to such extremes.

After lunch, Michele takes me on a speedy tour of her favorite areas, driving through a busy intersection, turning her head this way and that, past the Bay Shore golf course, down Collins Avenue, pointing out the Royal palms that Fisher planted and the rows of Australian pines along Pinetree Drive originally planted as windbreakers for the tropical fruit growers, the Pygmy date palms, frangipani, hibiscus, oleander, poinciana... She knows the names and has stories to tell about every plant. I begin to see it all through her eyes: the early houses, the lawns and gates and pretty stucco facades, as if the ugly thirty-story condos had never been built.

To outsiders like myself Miami always seemed stuck in a continual state of flux, seasonal, transient, enchanting yet frustratingly shallow, passing through its gaudy phases like a restless adolescent, never growing up for real. My first time here was in 1967 with a school friend and I remember buying a pair of rose-tinted sunglasses and seeing everything as if in a dream: the new highways and shopping malls, the heart-breaking hulks of the old Deco hotels along Ocean Drive with their crumbling walls and folding aluminum chairs out front. All the South Beach hotels have now been restored but I liked them better then, in ruin, better left to the imagination.

On my walk down the beach this morning I overheard a dozen different tongues—right at the water's edge—Spanish, Brit-English, Dutch, Swedish, German, Japanese, Italian. You look at the water and say, how lovely, but there's something lurking under all the international hype. It's the underside of the tropical resort theme, beneath the smell of the *Bain de Soleil* and the margaritas there's a sordid history of rum-running, sugar exploitation, salvagers, slave trade, yellow fever, the whole bloody southern tragedy. Maybe it grabs you the first night, but more likely it comes the third or fourth night when the novelty of the place is wearing thin. It's something fretful and hollow at the same time—something almost mad—a loosening of identity as if a part of you had been kidnapped by the saw grass and palmetto. It's in Wallace Stevens's "angering" of plant life that Michele recited under the Pigeon tree. It often comes after a late dinner, after a bit too much to drink. You notice the sound of the wind, a low-pressure front, the slap of waves against a bulkhead. It's there in the sweetness of the blossoms and the clacking sound of leaves in the dark. Later that night you dream about a perfect lagoon with pink sands and clean water. You can see everything beneath the surface: the coral reef, the schools of fish, the spooky roots of the mangroves. By morning, when the sun blazes on the white walls, it's almost forgotten.

On first glance, Miami Beach appears to be a series of arbitrary improvisations. To the authors of this book, it is a real place with a real history and a real culture. There were the woodsmen who came early in the 20th century to gather mangrove bark for tannic acid. There was also torpor, disease, and hurricane, the ultimate leveler. Something happens to people when they venture into this latitude. Even the most Presbyterian sensibilities come unhinged. The names of the streets and marinas tell their story: the dreamers, visionaries, architects and real estate moguls who had the will and capital to see their schemes realized, their viaducts and road works, their fabulous waterworks, sparkling lagoons and romantic islets. They were the ones who knew how to drain the swamps, sweep away the rack and ruin, spray the mosquitoes, and plant pristine English lawns and golf courses. They built grandiose structures in confectionaries of Spanish stucco as foils to the sun, with exotic gardens right at the water's edge despite the warnings, despite storm surge and malaria. Flagler builds his railway to infinity. It isn't enough for him to merely reach Miami. He has to force his folly all the way to Key West and would have crossed the sea to Havana if his engineers hadn't quit.

John Collins plants avocado and mango trees, builds a canal and (in 1913) two-and-a-half miles of wooden planks that connect Miami Beach to the mainland. Carl Graham Fisher, Babbitt from Indianapolis, comes on vacation but is too restless to sit still. He envisions a sweeping panorama of swaying palms, glittering boulevards and gondolas gliding across the bay towards Venetian-style palazzos. He leaves town but soon returns with all of the dredging equipment, steam rollers, and sump pumps he had used to build the Lincoln Highway. He also brings along a pet elephant named Carl. One of the machines has rotary knife-blades specially designed to cut through the gnarly mangrove roots. After that, the ugly stumps are covered with a million tons of sand pumped from the bottom of the bay. Within months the Nautilus, first of the big hotels, opens with its own polo field. Miami Beach soon becomes the gauge of market volatility, constantly fluctuating in value. The Crash of '29 is followed by years of bankruptcy and the post-war retirement ghetto with its littered beach and faded splendor. But in the 1960s a rat-pack eleganza returns with Morris Lapidus's Eden Roc and Fontainebleau hotels and his Cubist streetscape for the Lincoln Blvd. promenade. In the 1980s, the city finds an unexpected new identity with the first episodes of *Miami Vice* and new buildings by Arquitectonica and the restoration of South Beach's hotels, freshly painted in Neco-wafer pastels.

Both of the authors grew up here and understand the city's oddly tangled narrative as well as anyone. Oka Doner is an artist inspired by nature: sea wrack, shells, roots and husks, who gathers and arranges, redraws, carves in wax, casts in bronze. Wolfson is an inveterate collector who started with hotel keys but soon graduated to the ephemera of propaganda,

over a lifetime gathering a subjective accumulation of "art-infested historical documentation," as he once described the unique collection that became the Wolfsonian Museum. "I see myself as an archeologist—unearthing evidences, unraveling clues, amassing testaments to our civilization… I collect; therefore, I learn."

Michele's father moved here in 1935. Wolfson's forefathers go back even further. Joe Wolfson was shipwrecked, a victim of Key West's professional wreckers. Louis Wolfson built the first sidewalk in Key West and served on the City Council. Wolfson's father, Mitchell I, moved to Miami in 1915 and became a prodigy in the real estate business. Both of their fathers became major players in the growth of the city, their careers a mix of politics and entertainment. They both served, at different times, as mayor. One owned theaters. The other was a Harvard graduate with a vital law practice, who served as a judge. Miami Beach offered escape from the harsh winters of the north, growing block by block off bronchial infections, but also as an escape from the Calvinist work ethic. Here one could learn how to relax and take time off, swimming, fishing, lying on the beach. It wouldn't come easily for a generation of immigrants who slaved for every penny but there were the hotels and nightclubs and the sense that an elaborate production was being carefully orchestrated behind the scenes. Miami Beach grew as a city of theater: the theater of the beaches, the theater of the avenues, the theater of the canals and lagoons.

The present book is an interwoven thatch of personal reflection, confession, and family history, as well as information on flora and fauna, architecture, geology, fashion and social history, memorabilia, letters, flowers, women's hats, celebrity photos, newspaper clippings, blueprints, and family snapshots. Like Stevens's "Nomad Exquisite," it reconfigures the prevalent mythology that defines this place of promise and passing fad, this place that has meant so many different things to so many different people.

Alastair Gordon is the author of several books, including *Weekend Utopia: Modern Living in the Hamptons*, *Beach Houses: Andrew Geller*, and *Naked Airport*. He is a contributing editor to *House & Garden* and *Dwell* magazines. His articles have been published in *The New York Times*, *Architectural Digest*, *Condé Nast Traveler*, *Vanity Fair*, and *Town and Country*.

Mermaid's Shaving Brush
Life-sized *algae penicillus capitatus*, a common plant of the calm shallows characteristic of the Continental Shelf beyond Miami Beach's sandy shoreline.

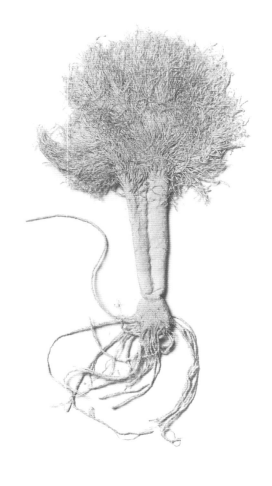

Preface

Miami Beach: The Past and Future Perfect

Miami Beach, Blueprint of an Eden is the story of an extraordinary time and place. It is the concurrent stories of two families placed by destiny in a position to tell them: the Wolfsons, and the Okas. Miami Beach has long been public property, well advertised and of easy access. This book takes it into the realm of private property, thereby giving it a private reading, an intimate touch, by which Miami Beach's strengths and absurdities are equally open to view. Through letters, a personal narrative is established that reveals Miami Beach as living experience.

The authors maintain the objectivity of anthropologists, who honor their material even as they dissect it and place it on the historical record. The book illuminates actual documents—maps, blueprints, schematics, recipes, sheet music, photographs—setting only one limitation: the use of intimate family archives. Most of the people, sights, events and structures articulated in these pages were part of the fabric of our families.

But unlike anthropologists, the authors are inseparable from what is presented. With respect and a great sense of celebration, we share our insights as to what it was like to grow up in an atmosphere that time would render mythical.

Michele Oka Doner and Mitchell Wolfson Jr.

October 2005

Eden in View
Site and Materials

"Man dwells naturally
within the tropics,
and lives on the fruit
of the palm-tree;
he exists in other parts of the world,
and there makes shift
to feed on corn and flesh."

Linnaeus, 1753[1]

Previous spread:
Palm seeds bursting forth from an open spathe.

The **coconut palm** was named *Cocos nucifera* by Linnaeus in 1753. **Palm trees** were belatedly added to the study of botany. In the first place, the discipline was initiated and carried out in northern climes. The tropics, though accessible by boat, were still considered remote and the distance created dilemmas. Any palm specimens retrieved were shriveled and dried during the long journey back to the home port. The nature of the palm leaf, several feet in length and much larger than an ordinary leaf, such as oak or elm, created an additional obstacle.

Dear Michele,

What the devil are ooids? Alas, Michele, one more
question I can't answer. But past times on Miami
Beach are for me vague images at best. How little
I recognize, how much I want to revisit it all.
Sometimes I hardly feel I was really there. But I
was, we were. Let's see if we can't help each other
remember the scenery or, as you point out, the sets,
of this grand concoction. I do recall the Miami
Beach Nursery. Did it really all begin with Japanese
gardeners inventing our own Eden on top of billions
of tiny egg-like particles bound together by
limestone? Are these spherical sand grains
mysteriously glued together our main support? Seems
pretty fragile to me! And then what? That gigantic
thermostat out our windows--the Gulf Stream that
shapes our existence? A great incubator of life?
Is how we live really determined by CaCO3, H2O,
vitamin D, and the coconut palm? I can't take it.
I want people, costumes, glamour, sex, bushes,
industry, architecture, ideas, culture, politics.
Don't you have some sort of family archive? I do,
somewhere or other. Wouldn't it be fun to pull
together documentation that would reflect an
extraordinary time and place that just happens to
be our own? Let's try to tell the tale using the
concurrent stories of our two curious families,
colonists by destiny in this vast aquatic warming pan.

Does the sum of all these parts add up to an
emerging Eden? We shall see as we become introduced
to certain driving forces that gave shape to the
resulting encounter of man and woman with nature.

Micky

Primeval Eden

Miami Beach, overlooking Indian Creek, during the process of clearing the native scrub, c. 1918.

Miami Beach is an elongated north-south barrier sandbar deposited by ocean currents particle by particle, over the course of geologic time. Waves and the prodding action of the Trade Winds caused the sand to mound above sea level. Seeds arrived by air and drift, ultimately covering the island with salt-resistant trees and shrubs, mostly mangrove. The landscape also contained rattlesnakes, rats and mosquitos. A 1917 survey conducted by the Smithsonian Institution in Washington, D.C. noted the island of Miami Beach. The island was referred to as "Crocodile Hole" because its only defining characteristic was a crocodile hole located at Indian Creek south of Allison Island.[2]

Shige Tashiro, the Japanese gardener who took this photograph, arrived just in time to witness that this primeval physical condition would be forever altered. Before his eyes, the dense South Florida native hammock was cleared and the timber and brush were burned. Dredged from the bottom of Biscayne Bay, fill material was then added to build up the irregular swampy surface. Fertile muck was dug from the Everglades and floated to the site on barges. The new Miami Beach was a construct by humans and nature.

All of these events worked in favor of the subsequent planting. Dade County soil has a great advantage over the heavy clay soils of many tropical countries that cake in the dry weather or become soggy during the rains. The character of the new topsoil, with its local component of Florida quartz, made an ideal medium. The landscape changed radically and within a period of thirty-six months, profits were realized on the pumping, dredging, and filling. Soon, Miami Beach was inundated with investors, developers and consumers of the new real estate.

The saw palmetto (Serenoa repens) created a ground cover over much of the sand dune area. Its fragrant, ivory-white flowers produce a fine amber-colored honey, the most widely produced of all of Florida honeys.

Magnificent Mangrove: Wonder of the Tropics

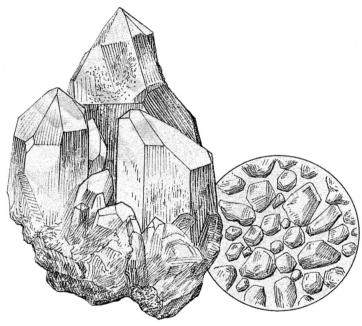

Recipe for Sand
Mix equal parts
of fine shell
and fine quartz grains.
Pack fairly firmly.

Left:
Dade County Soil Bar
Soils are created on
the surface of this earth
from the weathered
remains of rocks,
minerals and organic
matter. Dade County's
soil is primarily quartz
sand beds mixed with
pulverized sea shells
and deposited in
layers over the oolitic
limestone substructure.
This soil column is a
three-foot-deep core of
well drained calcareous
sand extracted from
Dade County by
the Department of
Agriculture for the State
of Florida in 1960.
The gray tone of the
soil profile indicates
the lack of humus or
other organic matter
characteristic of Miami's
local soil. In addition
to a superlative climate,
Florida's soils are
considered her greatest
natural resource.[3]

Far left:
Castles in the Sand
Quartz sand is
composed of loose,
unconsolidated minute
grains of crystalline
silica. Varying in hue
from opaque white to
clear, quartz sand is the
most abundant surface
material in the State
of Florida. The beaches
of Miami Beach are
composed of equal
parts of fine shell and
fine quartz grains and
are considered fairly
steep. However, the
sand is packed firmly,
making what is available
usable and, fortunately,
the island of Miami
adjoins a gently sloping
broad flat which creates
a generous spread of
shallow water.

Opposite:
A tangle of virgin
mangrove, Miami
Beach, 1918

Mangroves are the
primary evergreen
hardwood composing
South Florida's
distinctive hammocks,
those tree islands
surrounded by
contrasted vegetation.
Red mangrove
(Rhizophora mangle)
is one of the wonders
of the tropics, uniquely
adapted to its saline
environment. The
mangrove begins life in
a curious manner. The
seed germinates on
the tree itself, a stout
structure sometimes
as thick as a pencil. It
grows downward, until
sheer weight dislodges
the seedling. It plunges
into the mud or water.
The seedling's flesh
contains abundant
food reserves, and a
mangrove seed can
remain viable for many
months, drifting from
one locale to another.
The tip of the seedling
has a profound hook.
Assisted by the
pronounced curvature
of the seed's graceful
form, the hook reaches
into the substrate and
establishes itself as a
vertical entity. As the
seed grows into a
shrubby tree with aerial
prop roots, the
mangrove provides
protection for the shore
during hurricanes.
These trees accumulate
detritus from tides and
storms in their network
of roots, establishing
a dialogue between the
intricate root system
and the ebb and flow of
mud, sand, and stones.
This accumulation of
flotsam and silt causes
the waters around the
mangrove to become
shallower and shallower
until the sea bottom is
finally converted into
new land. When
undisturbed in dense
pure stands, the
mangrove can grow to
substantial heights.

Origins of an Eden

Where is Miami Beach? Latitude 25°48' north, the sandbar is parallel to great civilizations of luxury and glamour, ancient Thebes and Luxor in the Valley of the Nile, and is four hundred miles south of San Diego, California. Isotherms, the imaginary lines connecting places with the same mean temperature, extend even further, to the hanging gardens of Babylon on the banks of the Euphrates, through Arabia to Karachi, Pakistan. Miami Beach is endowed with 359 days of sunshine each year and is less subject to the extremes of weather than Cannes and Nice on the Riviera or Naples in the Mediterranean. Disconcerting changes from heat to cold are practically unknown. The average temperature during the winter months is 68°, only 12.4° less than summer.

What, then, makes Miami Beach an Eden? South Florida is flat. As a result, it conserves much of its rainfall in a high water table. This source of water supplies enough moisture to produce the exuberant tropical growth associated with places having twice as much rain. South Florida's bedrock is porous limestone able to absorb and hold water. Roots of trees and shrubs dig deeply into this rock and tap a source of constant moisture, an asset during any dry period. And the Gulf Stream glides by, keeping nights warm enough to sustain lush tropical growth.

The Gulf Stream, a river in the Ocean, is fifty miles wide as it pours through the Straits of Florida, and moves by Miami Beach at about four miles per hour. Two thousand feet deep and one thousand times the size of the Mississippi, North America's great river, the Gulf Stream flows from the Gulf of Mexico to the distant shores of the North Atlantic and Western Africa, and never mixes with the ocean. It is home to over six hundred varieties of fish as well as many other pelagic treasures. Three quarters of a century ago, the National Geographic Society sent John Oliver La Gorce to survey this "gift of fishes."[4] La Gorce concluded that practically one fifth of the entire fauna of the American continent north of Panama was contained in the warm water of the Gulf Stream.[5]

Beautifully drawn map depicting the powerful cycle of the Gulf Stream, a river in the ocean, 1921.

"Sun makes climate and climate with the aid of Trade Winds makes Florida. She tilts her sunburned nose so far down into the tropics that only here, in all the United States, can you pick coconuts from their lofty habitat—that is if you can climb well.

Life here has a different tempo, a sort of tropic rhythm. Sun, sand, the blue sparkling waters of the Gulf Stream, blossoms of every hue and waving palms bring a sense of luxury even to the masses."[6]
John Oliver La Gorce

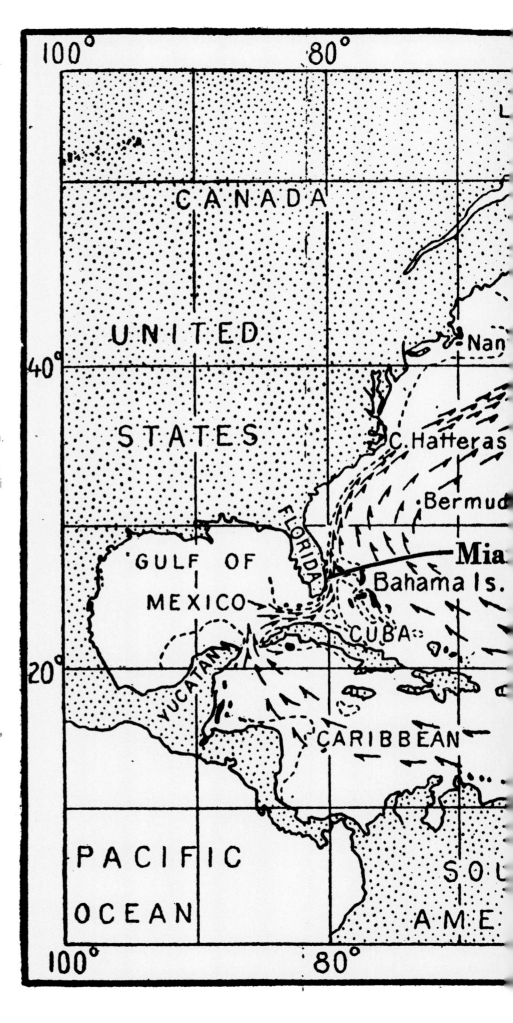

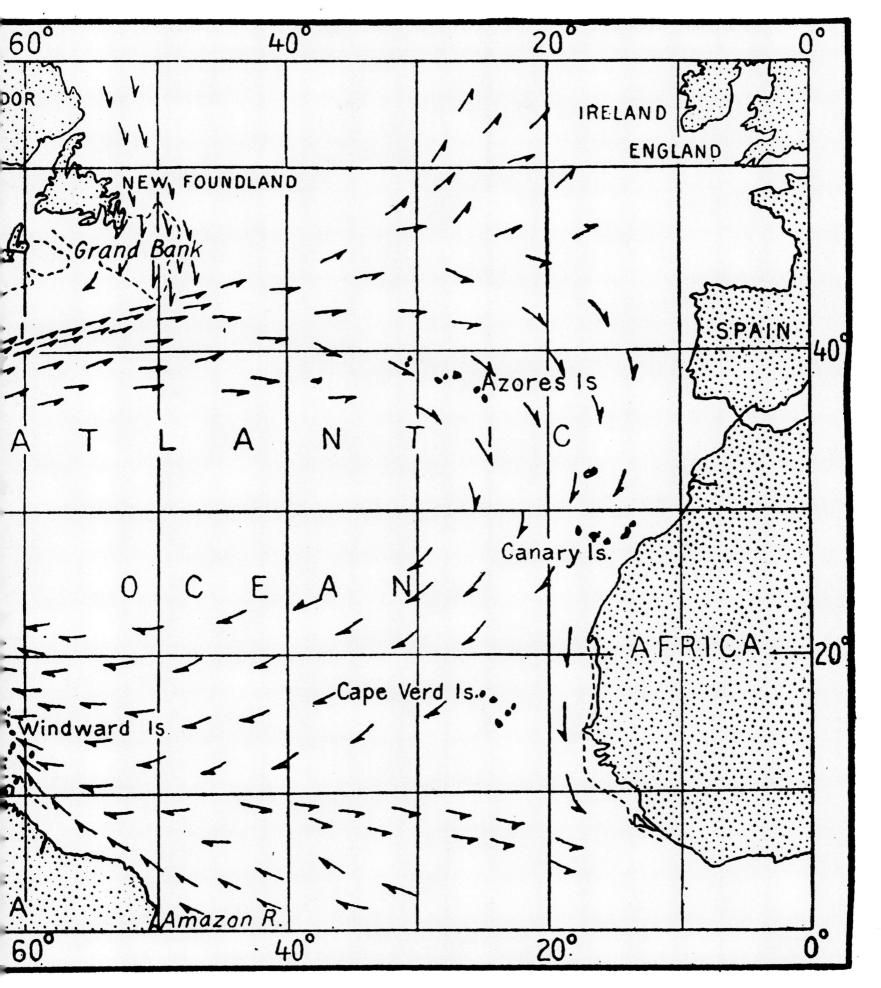

60°　　　　　　　40°　　　　　　　20°　　　　　　　0°

DOR

NEW FOUNDLAND

Grand Bank

IRELAND

ENGLAND

A T L A N T I C

SPAIN

40°

Azores Is

O C E A N

Canary Is.

AFRICA　20°

Cape Verd Is.

Windward Is.

Amazon R.

60°　　　　　　　40°　　　　　　　20°　　　　　　　0°

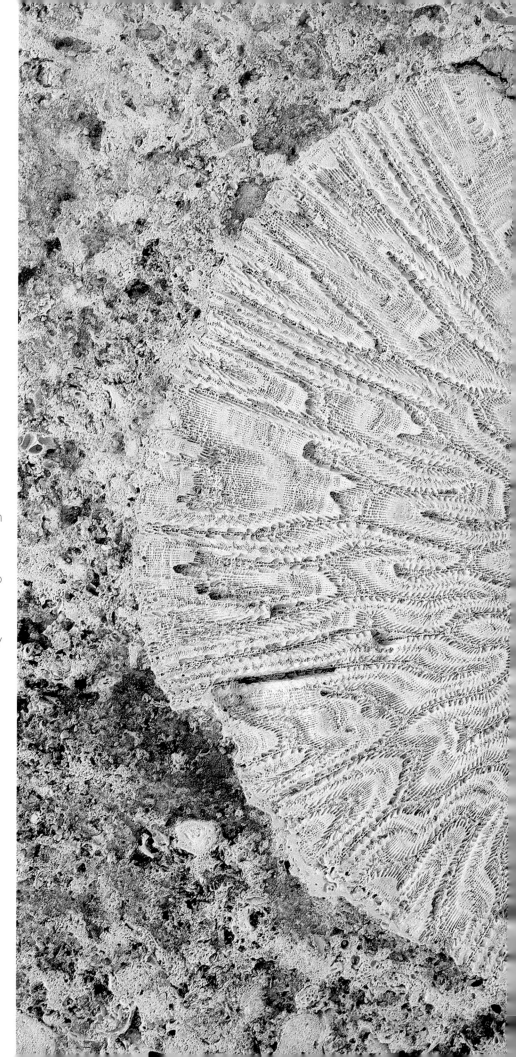

A Virtual Limestone Factory

Ooids are ovoid, spherical grains, microscopic building blocks for the fossil oolitic limestone ridge that is the bedrock of much of Dade County. This shape is formed by rolling along the bottom of the ocean. The shiny nature of the grains results from abrasion polish. Loose ooids are commercially dredged from the ocean for their mineral content. Considered by futurists to be an important resource, ooids are incorporated in cement production, the agricultural and glass industries, and animal foods.

Slivered and examined under a close-up lenses; the structure of the ooids emerges. The thin growth laminae form over a nucleus at the center of the grain. The dark zones are aragonite, a mineral-like limestone composed of calcium carbonite, but with a different crystal system. Many marine algae and sea shells are mostly aragonite. The mollusks secrete their fragile skeletons of tiny aragonite crystals, forming a fine-grained mud when the creature dies and their shells decompose.

Ooids, named for their resemblance to tiny fish eggs, begin as loose and unconsolidated jots. They are formed by chemical precipitation when deposition of calcium attaches itself around the tiny particles. These particles in turn deposit themselves layer upon layer on the ocean bottom. The ocean is turbulent, and its currents run in many different directions. The ooids layers flow in accordance, creating a sedimentary rock with a visual rhythm. South Florida waters produce more limestone than any other part of the country, a virtual limestone factory manufacturing sedimentary rock.

Fossilized brain corals are found in quarries from Key Largo to as far north as the Palm Beach and Broward County line. Twelve kilometers east of the Miami Canal, at the County line, the Griffen quarries contain exquisite remains of great coral masses and ancient reef life. This is arguably the most important fossil repository of the Middle Pleistocene Era in the United States.

Essence

oo: egg

lite: stone, mineral, fossil

id: body, particle

Previous spread:
Egglike ooids, building blocks of Dade County bedrock

Right:
A close-up, cross-section of fossilized brain coral *(Meandria)* imbedded in oolitic limestone (commonly known as keystone or coral rock). This is an example of the building block often used in Miami's architecture of the 1920s and 1930s. This example is from the Bass Museum of Art, designed in 1930 by Russell T. Pancoast as the original Miami Beach Public Library.

Far right:
Miami Beach in the Pleistocene Era
This map depicts southern Florida about one million years ago, during the Pleistocene era. The black contour line represents the outline of present-day Florida.

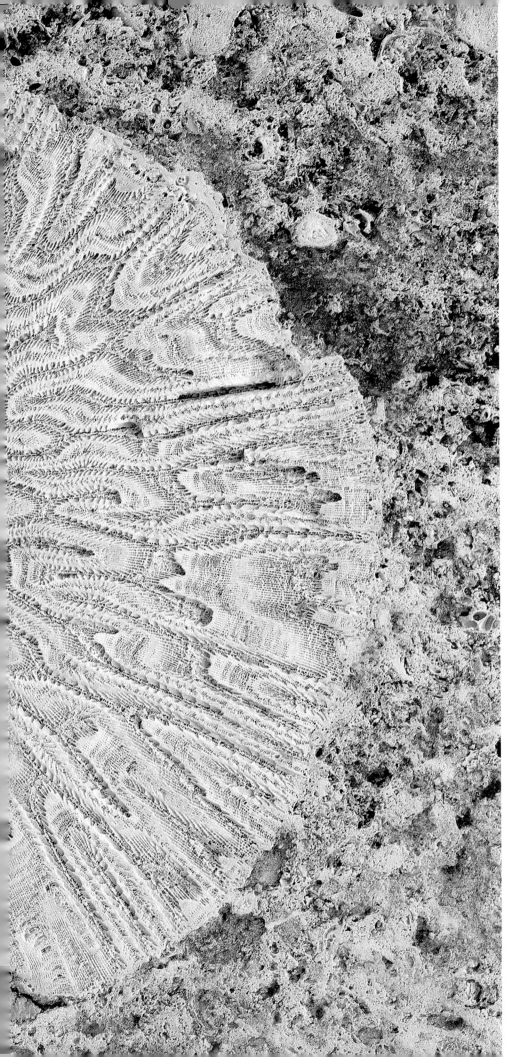

One Million Years Ago

Unlike Ordovician Ohio, lower Florida's origins are recent, belonging to the Pleistocene period, the latest of the earth's great geologic eras. At one time, all of the lower part of the State was below sea level. The Okeechobean Sea, a dominant feature, was connected to both the Gulf of Mexico and the Atlantic Ocean at that time.[7] The sea formed a template for the shape and structure of the modern Everglades. This body of water was graced, like an atoll, by a strand of tropical islands fringed with abundant growth of turtle grass in the clear, shallow, sun-warmed waters. Miami Island was the largest and best developed in the Eastern Archipelago that fronted Florida's seaboarc.

About ten thousand years ago, at the close of the Pleistocene or Ice Age, the waters began to recede and the State of Florida took its present form. Spectacular coral reefs grew in the tropical seas that surrounded the new peninsula. The reefs were enchantingly beautiful, composed of clusters of brain corals, colonies of star corals, and vast communities of finger corals. The reefs were home to large quantities of complex and curious shells as well. As the water continued its recession, the reefs were exposed to the air and dried out. The corals died, decomposed, and ocean currents scattered the debris. Layers of ooids from the ocean bottom became new dry land. Rainwater trickled in between the exposed ooid grains, dissolving some of the lime. This in turn re-precipitated as a binding agent, cementing ooids, the coral rubble, and shells to form a solid rock. The ancient sea floor documents the wealth of species that flourished before the arrival of humans in this area, and the finite nature of all living things. Today, much of western Miami rests upon the remains of this vanished world.[8]

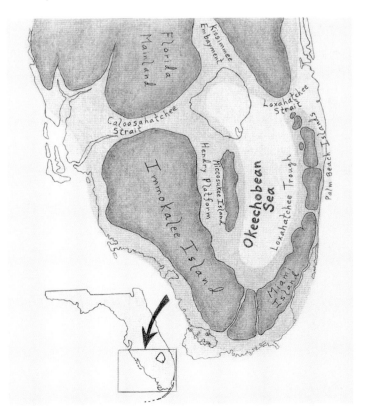

Transforming the Landscape

Pioneer gardener Shige Tashiro was born in the village of Kano, south of Tokyo, in 1880, the son of a Japanese silkworm farmer. He left Japan at the age of nineteen for the United States, settling first in California, where he acquired gardening knowledge and skill through apprenticeship and practical experience. In 1914, Tashiro was hired by pioneer settler General Samuel C. Lawrence to come to Miami and create a Japanese garden at Lawrence's seventy-acre farm, situated on the scenic rapids of the Miami River, two miles northwest of Miami.[9] Grapefruit, oranges, and tangerines already grew in profusion. It took Tashiro two years to complete the job, and in 1916 he crossed the wooden bridge to Miami Beach—which, when built in 1913, was the longest bridge of its kind in the world—to work for Carl Fisher, the visionary real estate developer who grew up on an Indiana farm. Tashiro's salary was $115 per month. A second gardener, Kotaro Suto, was hired by Fisher as well. He opened his own business, Suto Nursery, on Prairie Avenue. Both sons of the soil, Tashiro worked with Fisher to transform a sedimentary barrier island from native scrub to tropical paradise. By 1920 Miami Beach had taken on the allure of a luxuriant botanical garden and Tashiro returned to Japan with a letter of re-entry from Fisher to visit his ailing father and find a bride. He returned the following year with a wife to begin a family and a business, the Miami Beach Nurseries. The photograph of Shige Tashiro with his wife Kayo and their children, Jane, Herbert, Joseph and Tom, shows them surrounded by a dense thatch of tropical foliage on the site of the nursery approximately ten years after it opened.

The Tashiro Family
c. 1930

The **papaya** is a giant herbaceous plant sometimes called a melon tree or papaw. Commonly used as a breakfast fruit, the papaya contains papain, an enzyme long recognized in the tropics for its digestive action. In South Florida, the papaya is second only to the mango in popularity. It is most distinctive for its rate of growth and prodigious production. In the course of one year, a planted seed will transform into a shade-producing, fruit-bearing "tree" which can reach a height of twenty-five feet.

Clumping fishtail palms are the only palms whose leaves have multiple segments. The tree derives its name from the fan shape of the leaflets. In addition to its unique leaf, the Fishtail palm is notable for bearing its fruit in a series of clusters starting at the top of each stalk. An entire life cycle, from the protrusion of a spathe (containing the seeds), the flowering stalks, ripening fruits, and ultimately the red berries darkening, drying, and dying, can be visible at one moment in time.

A splendid small tree and a native Florida palm, *Coccothrinax argentata* has large fan leaves that are white or silver on the underside. These leaves are flexible and flash dramatically in the bright sunlight, making *Coccothrinax* quite desirable for ornamental plantings.

The red flower-like leaves of the **poinsettia** hide its true flowers. They are gathered in the center and resemble tiny green teapots with red lids and yellow spouts. The green leaves are hairy underneath and lobed in different ways. *To prevent wilting of the cut flower, the stems should be plunged at once into hot water and remain there until cool.*

Tashiro's Nurseries

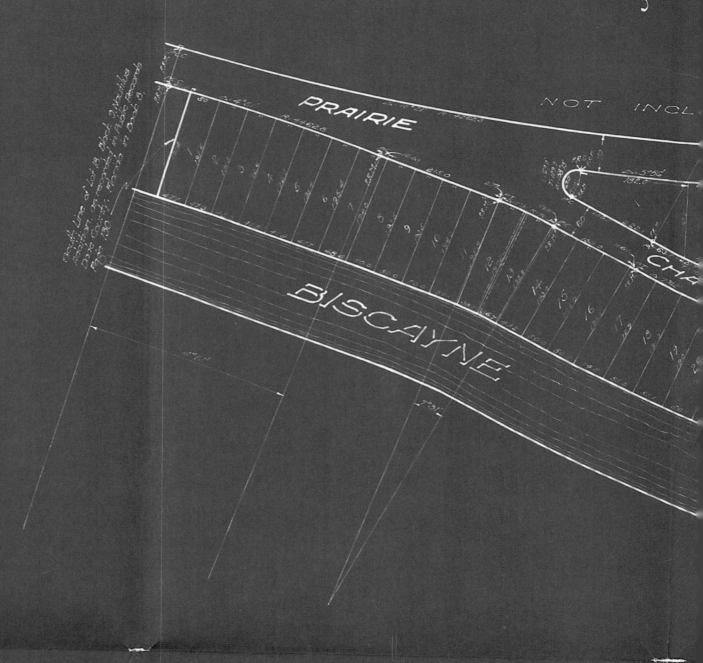

NURSERY SUBDIVISION
OF
MIAMI BEACH BAY SHORE CO.
MIAMI BEACH, FLORIDA
Being a subdivision of part of the Southeast quarter (SE¼)
of Section Twenty Two (22) Township 53 South, Range 42 E.
Dade County, Florida

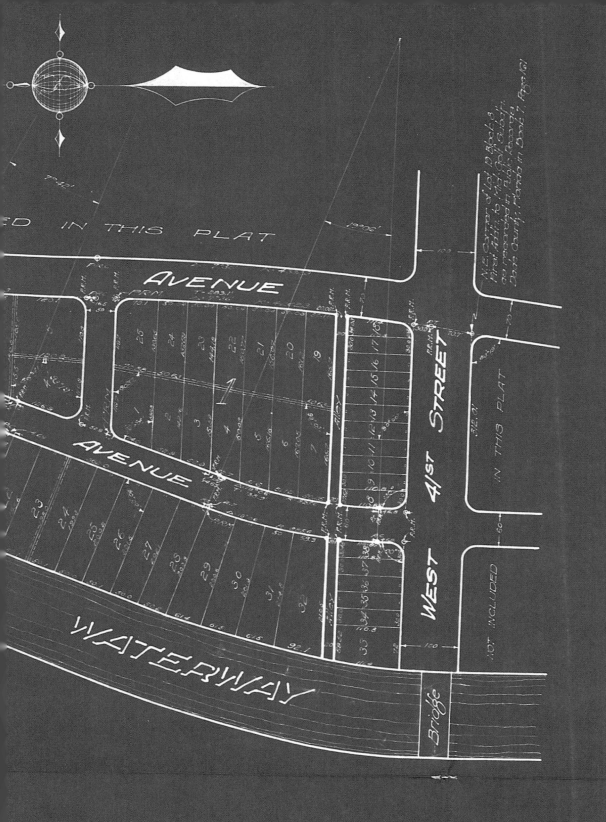

ED IN THIS PLAT

AVENUE

AVENUE

WATERWAY

WEST 41ST STREET

Bridge

IN THIS PLAT

NOT INCLUDED

A Manual for Living

To millions of people in today's tropical world, the coconut palm is the tree of life. It supplies all of their needs from birth to death. Every part of this tree fills a need. Trunks can become uprights in construction work, wood is made into useful articles, leaves roof native huts, and the hard shells of the nut provide drinking cups and buttons. In addition to these tangible provisions, the coconut palm nourishes the mind's eye. Its characteristic leaning cylindrical trunk, capped with a feathery crown of dark green arching leaves, is an icon of Paradise.

All parts of the coconut, one of the largest palm seeds in the world, are useful. The meat, called "copra," when dried, is converted to soap, margarine, and cooking oil. The flavorful coconut milk is also important for cooking and drinking. A multitude of products, including rope, brushes, and matting are derived from "coir," the husk of the coconut.

"Coir" and "Cairo" derive from the same root word. They evoke the beginning of recorded history, and suggest human interaction with and dependence on nature. After the husk has been removed, the coconut has three black dots and bears some resemblance to the face of a monkey.[10] The word "cocos" may have come from the Portuguese word for monkey.

The Miami Beach Nurseries opened in 1921. Located at Chase Avenue north of 41st Street, it occupied four city lots totalling approximately one and one-half acres. Shige Tashiro specialized in palms and bougainvillaea. *Bougainvillaea glabra* were easily propagated from cuttings, while the young royal palm *(Roystonea Elata)* specimens were brought in from the Everglades. Fast growing coconut palms could be started from seed. The more established Palm Beach also became a source for plants, and excursions for additional material as far afield as St. Augustine and even the Sea Islands of Georgia were not uncommon.

Tashiro provided landscaping services and assisted with the extensive plantings at the Vanderbilt estate on Fisher Island. As a nurseryman, he continued to concern himself with how plants would grow in the heat and moisture of the tropics. He began to address the issues of arrangement and placement of plant material. Instructive books such as *An Introduction to the Study of Landscape Design* by Henry Vincent Hubbard and Theodora Kimball, published in 1927 by the Macmillan Company, were acquired for his personal library.

Previous spread:
Blueprint of original site plan for the Miami Beach Nurseries, January 18, 1926

Above:
The Tashiro family with their Pontiac in front of the nursery A decade's growth of oleander *(Nerium oleander)* and Australian pine *(Casuarina equisetifolia)* is visible in the background. Banded wood containers filled with agave are ready for delivery.

Right:
Joe Tashiro hauls coconuts at Miami Beach Nurseries in his toy Mack truck.

How to Access a Coconut

Fresh coconuts are available year round in South Florida. A young nut has soft, jelly-like meat which can be eaten with a spoon. The mature hard meat is eaten in chunks or grated. Usually, a machete is used to remove the tough outer husk, for this milk bottle on the doorstep of humankind is not as accessible as a nursing mother's breast.

In past times, children growing up under coconut trees had to be resourceful. To open a coconut, the most often employed technique was to find hard ground such as a paved street or an uncommon sidewalk and hurl the coconut to the ground to crack the husk. When the husk broke open, a wedge of metal such as a screwdriver was inserted to pry the exterior shell from the giant seed.

Once the entire husk was completely removed, revealing a large beautiful hairy nut, the eyes were punctured with an ice pick and the sweet milk was drained into a cup. A hammer completed the job, cracking the inner structure to reveal the firm white meat inside.

Landscape for Sale
Lush vegetation at Miami Beach Nurseries includes coconut palm, royal palm, hibiscus (*Hibiscus Rosa-sinensis*), tropical hedge cactus (*Cereus peruvianus*) and agave. Most of these plants were grown in tubs to facilitate transplanting to new locations.

The royal palm is appropriately named. It grows rapidly, distinguished by a smooth, light grey trunk that appears more like a stone column than a living object. Its immense leaves, up to ten feet long, form a magnificent spreading crown that surmounts the trunk and adds to the royal palm's regal bearing. The majority of the old royal palms in South Florida were imported from Cuba in the 1930s. Royal palms thrive in the ideal conditions provided by South Florida's continuous warmth and a high water table. Those in the wild are now protected by conservation laws.

Rose of China ("*Psyche*" *Hibiscus Rosa-sinensis*) is the theme flower of the tropics and the most widely planted shrub that circles the equator. The hibiscus cross pollinates easily and seeds abundantly, creating a rainbow of colors with hundreds of named varieties that bloom year round. "*Psyche*," with small red flowers and ruffled petals, was one of the first varieties brought to the Miami area. *The radiant blossoms of the hibiscus last only one day but can be preserved for decoration at night by cutting the buds early in the morning, wrapping them tightly, and refrigerating until late afternoon. They can be displayed without water, a condition which allows them to occupy spaces without vases.*

Memories of Miami Beach

Do you remember when boats left Elser pier which was then located at the foot of Flagler St. in Miami, for the old docks on Miami Beach, due west of Hardie's Casino, which is now the foot of Biscayne St.? That was before the wooden bridge was built by Pioneer Collins.

On Sunday afternoons, many hundreds of Miamians would ferry across for their ocean dip at Smith's Casino or Hardie's Casino at South Beach. That was the finest ocean beach in Southeast Florida in those days, and for that matter, still is the best beach for bathing in this section of the country.

Do you remember later the thousands of motorists who drove up Avenue "B" (now N. E. 2nd Ave.) turned right at the Garden of Eden (now N. E. 14th Ter. and 15th St.) to drive across the longest wooden bridge in the world, now the site of the Venetian causeway?

Do you remember how beautiful the green grass stood out on the Fisher golf course (now the City of Miami Beach Municipal course)?

Do you remember the swell bathing and swimming at Fisher's Casino (now the Everglades Cabanas, owned by Malone properties)?

Do you remember Peter Des-Jardins and Newt Roney and many others with their fancy diving and aquatic sports at Fisher's pool?

Do you remember the real estate "For Sale" sign on the lot across the street where the Roney Plaza is now located, which was there for a long time reading— "For Sale—This Entire Block $15,000"?

Do you remember the old city hall way down on South Beach—with T.E. James as mayor?

Do you remember the mangrove swamps and the mosquitos, the lack of drinking water, the tough summers and a host of other pioneering problems?

It is truly difficult to believe what has happened to Miami Beach in 25 years unless one has actually seen the transition from a mangrove swamp and ocean beach that has grown to the magnificent city that is now Miami Beach.

No magic wand ever waved by fairy godmother was ever able to make the magic change that transpired in 25 years on the spot that is now known as the city of Miami Beach. Fully aware of our city's problems, exhorted by my heritage of birth in southeast Florida, stimulated by the growth and attractiveness of my home town and fully conscious of the possibilities of Miami Beach over the next 25 years, I am dedicating my effort, my time and whatever ability I might have towards the complete fulfillment and realization of that wonderful dream visioned by the founders of our city, those great pioneers whom we must salute and revere on the 25th anniversary of the finest spot in the world.

Mitchell Wolfson

Miami Beach Tropics
The Newspaper of the World's Playground
Friday, March 19, 1940

"No magic wand ever waved by fairy godmother was ever able to make the magic change that transpired in twenty-five years."
Mitchell Wolfson

The Miami Beach Pier, c. 1916

Family Tendrils
People Take Root

Previous spread:
Mockingbirds and Orange Blossoms, n.d., india ink and handmade water-based colors on silk, 30" x 47." Painted by Frances Wolfson, Collection of Florida House, Washington, D.C.

Below:
Germinating mangrove seedling, washed up on Miami Beach shoreline

The **mockingbird** (*Mimus polyglottos*, meaning a mimic of many tongues) was nominated by the school children of Florida as State Bird and was approved by the Legislature on April 23, 1927. It is abundant throughout the State and well loved for its cheery, rollicking song and its ability to accurately mimic the call of other birds. Though wild, the mockingbird is seldom found far from the habitations of humans. The bird nests in bushes that surround Florida homes and in vines that screen Floridian porches. In the early 1930s, the Bok Singing Tower in Central Florida staged a competition between the mockingbird and European nightingale. The issue to be decided was which creature was the better singer. When the caged, imported nightingales began a hymn new to American ears, Florida mockingbirds adopted it at once and made it their own![1]

Oranges were once the fruit of gods, emperors, kings, aristocracy and finally ordinary people.[2] Oranges arrived in Florida in about 1565 with early settlers, and were disseminated by Native Americans scattering seeds as they ate the fruit. Great quantities of rain in the state prevent a thick albedo, the white part of the skin, from forming. So an orange grown in Florida has a thin, tight skin and is heavy with juice (unlike California oranges which have thicker skins that peel off for easy eating). Florida surpassed California in the 1940s to become the country's leading orange producing state. Oranges and orange blossoms have long been symbols of springtime and love. The seventeenth-century poet of paint, Peter Paul Rubens, depicted these botanical images on a large panel now in the Alte Pinakothek in Munich, Germany. Painted early in his new marriage, the canvas is a visual love letter. Tubs of orange trees fill the picture, alluding to the tradition of brides commonly carrying this fragrant blossom as an emblem of redemption from the sins of Eden.

Bees regard the orange blossoms as one of nature's golden sweets. The orange blossom honey they produce is light amber in color, heavy in body, and contains the aroma of a grove in bloom.

MITCHELL WOLFSON JUNIOR

5030 NORTH BAY ROAD · MIAMI BEACH, FLORIDA 33140

Dear Michele,

My people seem to have floated up from Key West quite naturally.
The Wolfson family story as seen by its heirs is an undramatic series of
events which first finds them there, now has them here. Standard evolutionary
progress as life that began on Pine Tree Drive moves almost imperceptibly to
Meridian Avenue under the shadow of the Second World War, and ultimately
flows with long established equanimity into North Bay Road.

Your family, I understand, arrived by train in 1935, motivated by the crash
of 1929 as much as by Uncle Eddie's rheumatic fever. Among those who built
the cityscapes we know, motivations faded fast in the grip of new realities.
If the Wolfsons admitted theirs to be as simple as more customers for dry
goods in Miami than in Key West, they never recounted what surely must have
been the excitement of change with all its doubts, pains and surprise.
Anywhere else in the South might have served them just as well. They already
had a foothold in Miami, and greater opportunity seemed close at hand. So
Miami it was.

You've told me the story of your grandfather. How, from his beginnings in
the Ukrainian woods and years spent in Manhattan, Miami Beach became the
great enchantress on sight with all its melodramas, sun, surf, and the
cornucopia of the tropics. When you contrast him with my forebears, we
realize how families of such disparate origins might find themselves in the
same place on the same geological stratum at the same time. For all that,
Michele, what should be of interest to us is not the saga of dissimilarities
but the strange perceptions others have of both our unclassifiable parents
and of us. No doubt we'll find that, energetic or passive, farsighted or
content, temperamentally reserved or openly loving, the players are
personalities more complex than we'd ever guessed.

In photographs, your mother seems informal, dramatic and extroverted; mine
self-contained, ceremonial and of another age. Both of our fathers look
sociable, prosperous and comfortably focused. How much of what seems is
true?

The Wolfsons

Previous spread:
A charming Wolfson family portrait used for campaign press during Mitchell Wolfson's 1941 race for Miami Beach City Councilman. Informally posed on the lawn of the Wolfson home on North Meridian Avenue, Mitchell Wolfson is seated with Frances Louise in his lap. Mrs. Frances Wolfson, in a daisy print dress with ruffles at the shoulder, a classic style of the 1940s, holds Mitchell Wolfson Jr., with Louis II at her right.

Destined to Bloom in Plaster
Blossom detail from the auditorium plaque, Carib Theater, Michael J. DeAngelis, 1950. A sensuous rendering of an exotic fantasy flower destined to bloom in plaster of Paris. The animated central projection, a pistil surrounded by stamen, has been expressed in rapturous detail.

The mathematical underpinnings of nature's design have been captured in the double spiral pattern known as *phyllotaxis*. The petals are exquisitely detailed with wavy lines, creating an illusion of softness.

Mitchell and Frances Wolfson

Mitchell Wolfson's ancestors arrived in Florida in the late nineteenth century. At that time there was no Miami and no Tampa. Jacksonville was a very small city. Key West contained approximately thirteen thousand people—the largest population in the state. Uncle Joe Wolfson was shipwrecked near Key West en route to Texas or New Orleans (the family is uncertain), and found himself rescued by wreckers—professional salvagers and predators. He wrote his brother Louis in New York, "Key West looks like a very nice city for a young man to get started in." The Mallory Steamship Line was the only way to get to Key West. There were no roads, and no railroads. It was an era of the Barefoot Mailman delivering both paper and travelers to the outpost that would become Miami.

Life was good in Key West, although it was hard. Key West is just a small island, one mile by three miles. Drinking water was a scare commodity. No meat was available, and few fresh vegetables. But there were plenty of fish, conch, key limes, avocados and mangos. There was yellow fever, typhoid fever, and no vaccinations. Louis Wolfson caught and survived both diseases. He prospered as a merchant and built the first sidewalk in Key West. Elected to the City Council in 1910, he instituted a tradition of public service for succeeding Wolfson generations.

Mitchell Wolfson, was born in Key West in 1900, a Child of the Century. By then Louis was successful, operating the House of Fashion on Duval Street. When Mitchell was fifteen, the Wolfson clan moved to Miami and established the East Coast Wholesale Corporation. They settled in a subdivision appropriately named "Garden of Eden" on Bougainvillea Court.[3]

Miami was a thriving community. The Great Florida Frost of 1894-95 pushed energy, economic growth and speculation further south in the State. The Spanish-American War, though fought in Cuba, had a ripple effect in the entire Caribbean basin. Miami became an important site for army camps and the industries required to sustain the conflict. It was time for the railroad to come to Miami. Julia Tuttle, considered the founding mother of the city, picked orange blossom sprigs, fruits, and vegetables and sent them to Henry M. Flagler, railway mogul, thereby demonstrating that no frost had kissed Miami's produce. Flagler responded by laying down tracks and extending the Florida East Coast Railway. A year later, Miami had access to the country at large.[4]

Wolfson, when still in his teens, displayed a magic touch in real estate. He accumulated properties in strategic locations. Under age, he had to use his mother's name, Rosa, to close his real estate deals. During this period, an event occurred that was to change the course of Wolfson's life. His sister Zenia married Sidney Meyer, a motion picture executive who worked for Fox Film Corporation in Chicago. When Zenia grew homesick for her family in Miami, Meyer joined the Wolfson family business. Dry goods turned out to be less exciting than film, and Meyer soon convinced Mitchell Wolfson to go into the motion picture business and build the grandest movie palace Miami had ever seen. They formed the WOlfson-MEyer-Theater COmpany, later known as Wometco, which grew to become one of America's leisure time corporate giants.

Frances Wolfson née Frances Louise Cohen was born December 16, 1906, the only child of Adolf and Teresa. He was of Yankee stock—though it was never spoken of by the family—and she, from a long line of prominent German Jews. In the 40s Frances took up Christian Science, not as an alternative but as a supplement to her inherited spiritual background. Her great, great, great, grandparents came to the United States in the late eighteenth century and settled in the New Orleans, Mobile, and Pensacola Gulf Coast area. Attractive, talented, and charming, she led a brilliant and remarkable life. As if inhabiting a prism, she reflected the multifarious values of her world. The times were fortunate, the protocol strict, the form classic.

Frances Wolfson painted, with great charm, Florida's state bird and flower. She discovered painting late in life. Drawn to the implicit order and unity of the Eastern tradition, Frances immersed herself in China's art and philosophy. Through the brushes she found a means to incorporate and reinvent her environment, her love of nature, and the subtleties of Florida's natural beauty. *Mockingbirds and Orange Blossoms*[11] was given to Florida House, the only State house in Washington, D.C. Conceived in the southern tradition of hospitality, Florida House provides services to Floridians visiting and working in the Nation's capital.

**"The front door
opens, Mitch gives
a whistle and all
is right in the
world of Frances
Wolfson. . .
the wife of the
co-founder of
Wometco theatre
chain is now a
grandmother, but
her husband's
greeting whistle
means as much
to her today as
when they began
their life together
in 1926."**
Margaret Acer, society
columnist, Miami *News*,
Thursday, June 12,
1958.[7]

The Wolfson Home

Designed in the Mediterranean Revival style (also referred
to as Venetian Gothic) by architects Carlos B. Schoeppl
and George Maguolo for the Bohn family of Detroit,
Michigan, the Wolfson home was completed in 1937.
Wrought iron gates and grilles, tile floors and roofs, pecky
cypress brackets, arched door and windows opening
as well as exterior courtyards, loggias, and patios
characterized the style. Because the Bohns were in the
bronze casting business (Bohn Bronze and Brass),
significant bronze detailing and decorative metalwork
was installed throughout their winter residence.

Diverse influences converged to flavor the development of
Florida Mediterranean architecture. The style flourished
from 1915 through the 1930s, when travel was increasingly
accessible and architects toured the nation and Europe
for inspiration. World's Fairs, those important disseminators
of ideas and trends, introduced new innovations to
American audiences. The 1915 Panama Pacific
International Exposition in San Diego brought national
prominence to the Spanish Baroque style.

The first examples of the Mediterranean style in Miami are
credited to August Geiger. The same year as the Panama
Pacific International Exposition, he built Miami City Hospital,
a mission style structure nicknamed "The Alamo," and, a
year later, he built the Miami Beach Municipal Golf Course.
(see page 163). Applied decorations on these structures
are appropriated from southern California's adaptation of
Mexican, New Mexican, and Texan stucco facades.
The same year, the newly completed seventy-room Villa
Vizcaya created a sensation in Miami. Villa Vizcaya merged
Mediterranean, Italian Renaissance, and local building
materials into a unique hybrid. Vizcaya stimulated
developers and designers to arrange a new palette.

The Wolfson home drew from this palette. Dade County's
oolitic limestone is used extensively, beginning with the
entrance gate and facade, and providing numerous pavers
and steps throughout the gardens and courtyards. Some
of the oolite was tinted pale green, a popular color of the
1930s. Conjuring up the Mediterranean, windows and door
openings are arched. A wide balcony overlooks the waters
of balmy Biscayne Bay. Decorative glazed ceramics and
tiles are incorporated through the house, and terra cotta
tiles create a varied roof line. A courtyard and loggia
separate the main structure from the entrance.[6] The loggia
ceiling is supported by beams of Dade County pine.

The banyan tree *(Ficus
benghalensis)* is held in
high regard the world
over. Gautama the
Buddha is said to have
received Enlightenment
while seated under the
banyan tree. The tree is
composed of a central
trunk and numerous
auxiliary trunks to help
support the super-
structure. The multiple
trunks originate not from
the ground as most
trunks do but as aerial
roots which sprout from
the branches.

These grow down, taking root once they reach the nurturing soil. The banyan that dominates the entrance to the Wolfson home is unusual, for throughout the years most of these vine-like roots have been pruned. Frances Wolfson, student of oriental landscape painting, applied the spare lines and great strokes of this art to the shapes of her trees.

This banyan has a bonsai appearance. Rigorous pruning also removed additional weight from the crown of the tree, enabling it to survive several Florida hurricanes intact. The banyan tree is masterfully lit with flood lights to reveal its structure at night.

Dade County pine *(Pinus elliotti)* was culled from primeval forests that occupied most of the higher limestone land in the southern part of Florida. Dade County alone sustained one hundred and eighty thousand acres of pineland carpet. Cut down to provide timber for pioneer structures and clear land for fruit producing groves, today Dade County Pine is on the verge of extinction.

Impenetrably tough and termite resistant, when milled into planks of lumber, the wood is so resinously transparent that when held up to a light source the surroundings takes on an amber aura.

Phoenix reclinata, the Senegal date palm, has a slender trunk and long plume-like bright green fronds. Composed of hundreds of dagger-like leaflets, the fronds radiate at different angles, reflecting prism-like refractions of light.

The ti plant *(Cordyline australis)* resembles a giant feather duster and is native to Polynesia. This vertical stalk was recruited to landscape Miami Beach. The Ti not only evokes the tropics, but, jungle-like, can grow in the shade and shadow of a great tree.

The maleleuca tree was imported from Australia to assist in eliminating marshy areas in Miami and the Everglades. Its paper-like bark can be gently peeled into thin sheets. Once in hand, the layers can be separated again and again until the final product becomes quite refined. The tree now stands accused by ecologists of too rapidly spreading, forcing out native growth.

Framed in the archway to her formal dining room, the statuesque **Mrs. Wolfson** pauses on an Italian marble pedestal-like step. A pair of elaborate floral brocade curtains enhance the setting.

"Preview peek at the magnificent gown to be worn by Mrs. Mitchell Wolfson, Symphony Club President, at the Symphony Ball on January 14 is given to Ball Chairman Mrs. E.E. Dale Shaffer. Mrs. Wolfson's gown is a Christian Dior original of French Silk embossed brocade, of cocoa brown and dark green embroidered flowers, draped with a short trim." Social columnist Jeanne Gerrard's "Plumage on Parade," 1956

Opposite:
The front entrance to the Wolfson home, 1961. This archway is an example of the unique synthesis of South Florida style. It encompasses the Mediterranean arch, inlaid Moorishesque glazed tiles, inner and outer oolitic limestone rims as well as the oolitic limestone platform. A pair of classic polychrome urns flank the archway. Inside, the "Egyptian Female Dancer" waves her arms in a welcoming gesture. Her skin is white marble, her brief garb articulated bronze. The rhythm of the exterior and interior arches makes a pattern of shadows which add a dimension of depth to the dramatic entrance.

Procession of Arches
To the left of the central hallway is the entrance to the Grand Salon. The repetition of arches on the ceiling is echoed by the inlaid patterns in the stone floors. Extravagant marbles—silver and golden travertine—were imported to construct these floors.

Additional marbles are used as a framing device. They create a jewel-like sensation with inlaid diamond motifs. Formal curtains dress the windows, and patriarch Louis Wolfson observes it all from his framed visage on the wall.

Stylish Interiors

Fred Rank, an interior designer who migrated from Chicago, completed the interior furnishings and appointments. Rank was considered the most important interior designer to arrive on the Miami scene. Previously, the socially committed went to Palm Beach to find a vehicle of style. Rank studied at both Columbia University and The Art Institute of Chicago, and was a charter member of the American Institute of Decorators.

Venetian Gothic Library
The wide range of books included Jack Kofoed's *Moon over Miami*, a volume by Thomas Wolfe, travel books from tiny Key West to vast Russia, and two bound collections of Colonel Wolfson's letters home during his service in the U.S. Army during World War II.

Another dancing figure holds open the door, a bookend to the figure in the front entrance hall.

Vast Ice Box for a Hot Climate

An oversized kitchen with a view into the butler's pantry. The original marble and steel iceboxes, fabricated by Chrysler and Koppin of Detroit, were converted to modern refrigerators. Mrs. Wolfson was known as an outstanding hostess. In The Miami *Daily News* of May 1, 1957, the front page of the food section published her family recipes and lauded her style:

"A gracious hostess who serves dishes that were served in Florida by her mother, her grandmother and her great grandmother, is Frances Louise (Mrs. Mitchell) Wolfson, North Bay Road, Miami Beach. When Mrs. Wolfson entertained members of the Symphony Club recently, serving tea to 50 members of the organization after the business session (when she was re-elected president), the table was loaded with mouth-watering sandwiches and cakes made from recipes handed down from her forebears. Dishes and silver combined treasures she inherited and pieces she collected during her trips to various corners of the world. This too, is Miami; is Florida."

51

From the Wolfson Kitchen

It is rumored that Ada Brodus, a longtime Wolfson housekeeper, created most of the Wolfson dishes but for public record, Mrs. Wolfson appeared to be a hands-on cook.

Mrs. Wolfson's **pickled shrimp** can be made two days ahead.

The taste for fresh Florida fish stayed with Mitchell Wolfson long after his boyhood in the Florida Keys, and Frances enjoyed serving his favorite **baked red snapper**. Pensacola, Frances's childhood home, was once the State headquarters for the snapper fleet.[8] At one time, in fact, Florida produced half of the red snapper sold in the United States.

Mrs. Wolfson's **lime chiffon pie** showcases another Florida fruit star, the lime. A major Florida crop, Florida limes are abundant year round. Frances Wolfson makes use of the vitamin rich rind as well as the juice.

Pickled Shrimp

2/3 cup corn or safflower oil
1 teaspoon dry mustard
2/3 cup vinegar
3 bay leaves
2 limes, juiced
1/2 teaspoon cayenne pepper
1-1/2 tablespoons sugar
2 pounds shrimp
1 teaspoon dill seeds
1/2 large onion, sliced
1 teaspoon cracked black peppercorns
1/2 cup chopped fresh cilantro

Combine the ingredients, except the shrimp, cilantro and onion, in a saucepan and bring to a boil; simmer for ten minutes. While the sauce is simmering, peel the shrimp, and devein them by making a slit along the back or outside of the shrimp, lifting out the black vein, and discarding it. Rinse the shrimp and add them to the saucepan. Simmer very gently for three minutes (the shrimp will become rubbery if brought to a hard boil). Drain the shrimp, reserving the cooking marinade. In a large bowl, layer the onion slices and the shrimp, alternating until both are used up. Sprinkle the cilantro into the reserved hot marinade and pour over the mixture. Cover tightly with plastic wrap. Chill for about forty-eight hours.

Remove the shrimp from the marinade and serve on wooden picks, or slice and place on pumpernickel rounds decorated with fresh cilantro leaves.

6 hors d'oeuvre servings.

Baked Red Snapper

1 whole red snapper (about 5 pounds with head)
1 tablespoon lemon juice
4 tablespoons butter or margarine (1/2 stick) melted
1 tablespoon Worcestershire sauce
3 stalks celery, finely sliced
2 teaspoons sugar
1/2 medium onion, finely sliced
1 teaspoon Tabasco sauce
1 15-ounce can tomato sauce
Salt and freshly ground black pepper to taste
1 51/2-ounce jar pimentos, drained and sliced
1 lemon, sliced into wedges

Preheat oven to 350 degrees. Ask your fish man to gut and clean the fish, but leave the head and tail on. Rinse the whole fish and place in a roasting pan or baking dish, just large enough to fit the fish. Pour the butter over the fish. Combine the remaining ingredients, except the lemon wedges, and taste for seasoning. Add more Tabasco or sugar as needed. Salt and pepper to taste. Pour the sauce over the fish and bake for forty-five minutes. To test for doneness, stick the point of a knife into the middle of the fish and pull some of the flesh aside; it should be opaque, not translucent. If not done, bake five to ten minutes longer. It should take about ten minutes per pound to bake. To serve, remove the fish from the pan and cut two or three servings from the top side. Place on individual plates. Remove the bone and cut the second side into sections and place on plates. Spoon the sauce over the fish and serve, garnished with lemon wedges.

4 to 6 servings.

Remember, snapper jaws and throats are the richest and most delicately flavored part of the fish.

Frances Wolfson's Lime Chiffon Pie

1 15-1/2 ounce can sweetened condensed milk
1 tablespoon gelatin
3 eggs, separated
1/4 cup cold water
4-6 fresh limes, grated rind and juiced (1/2 cup)
9-10" graham cracker pie crust

In a medium-size bowl whip the condensed milk and egg yolks until thoroughly combined. Add the grated rind and lime juice. Soften the gelatin in the water in a metal measuring cup and place over low heat in a water-filled skillet until gelatin has dissolved. Stir the gelatin into the filling and spoon into the graham cracker crust. Refrigerate until set, at least two hours. This may be made a day ahead.

Pound Cake

2 cups butter
2 teaspoons vanilla
3 cups sugar
2 teaspoons almond flavoring
8 eggs, separated
2 jiggers (6 tablespoons) bourbon
3 cups flour
1/2 cup, or more, finely chopped pecans

Cream butter, gradually adding sugar and beat until fluffy; add egg yolks one at a time, continuing to beat until very light and fluffy. Be sure not to underbeat. Add flour along with flavoring and bourbon; fold in stiffly beaten egg whites. Grease a tube pan, line with waxed paper and spread in the bottom a layer of finely chopped pecans. This layer should be about one-fourth inch thick. Carefully pour in batter and bake in moderate oven (350 degrees Fahrenheit) one and one-half hours. Cool in the pan.

It is within the realm of possibly to take this already perfect pound cake a little bit further. The vanilla vine, a member of the orchid family, grows in Dade County.[9] Two species are native to the rich hammocks of lower South Florida, _V. eggersii_ and _V. articulata_.[10] The vine crawls freely over trees, clinging with its tenacious roots. If you can find these or the more readily available _Vanilla planifolia_, take the fresh vanilla bean, enclose it in a jar of sugar, and seal it tight. Within a week, the perfumed sugar is ready to be added to the pound cake.

Mary Randolph's 1824 cookbook, _The Virginia House-wife,_ was the first collection of what were considered to be American recipes, and included a recipe for pound cake. The book establishes a provenance for what has been a favorite dessert for American families for almost two centuries. Her recipes attempted to standardize classics, and poundcake has as many variations as the cook's palate or the location's peculiar ingredients.

Mrs. Wolfson's family **pound cake** increased the sugar and decreased the flour. This was a departure from the original pound cake recipe, which earned its name from a uniform measurement of ingredients: a pound of butter, a pound of sugar, a pound of flour. The incorporation of pecans adds a southern touch appropriate for the great-granddaughter of a soldier who fought for the Confederacy. Mitchell Wolfson also fondly recalled his mother Rosa's pound cake. Rosa used cashews instead of pecans. The African influence on American cooking is noteworthy, and one wonders if this influence is responsible for the introduction of nuts into pound cakes from southern kitchens.

"Floridian by Tradition: Modernizes 'Old South'

You'll want to try this very special Pound Cake. Mrs. Mitchell Wolfson cuts the first slice of fine grained and very tender beauty which would be recognized by guests who were served by her mother, grandmother and great-grandmother—four generations of Floridians! But the cake is new as tomorrow, wearing a crown of crunchy pecans that bake right in the pan with the batter."
Miami *Daily News* Food Section, May 1, 1957, by Berta Cochran Hahn

YOU'LL WANT TO TRY THIS very special Pound Cake. Mrs. Mitchell Wolfson cuts the first slice of fine grained and very tender beauty which would be recognized by guests who were served by her mother, grandmother and great grandmother—four generations of Floridians! But the cake is new as tomorrow, wearing a crown of crunchy pecans that bake right in the pan with the batter.

Varying The Mood

Some recipes, like the sandwich fillings that are seasoned "to taste" so that they seem to improve with each variation, are never reduced to written recipes but retain their basic ingredients through the years.

Cakes, sometimes baked without reference to the written word after long experimentation with quantities, sometimes written carefully in private ledgers and guarded so closely that recipes could only be obtained by marrying into the family, have become so standardized we can hope to produce a masterpiece the first time a recipe is used.

Easy success makes us forget the artistry that fashioned those original dishes and that is especially true of the Pound Cake which earned its name because ingredients in the first cakes were measured by the pound—a pound of butter, a pound of sugar, a pound of flour and a pound of eggs. The variation used by Mrs. Wolfson increases the sugar and reduces the amount of flour. The pecans are a novel touch that you'll really appreciate.

Chocolate cake is always popular and this Devil's Food recipe is another that you'll make until you, like the cooks of another generation, will not need the written recipe.

Petits Fours, like the sandwiches, are never twice the same, but follow the mood of a cook; only the basic batter is repeated. Frostings can be fondant or made with confectioners' sugar; variety is in the shape of cake pieces as well as in color and flavor of the frosting.

POUND CAKE

- 2 cups butter
- 3 cups sugar
- 8 eggs, separated
- 3 cups flour
- 2 teaspoons vanilla
- 2 teaspoons almond flavoring
- 2 jiggers (6 tablespoons) bourbon
- ½ cup, or more, finely chopped pecans

Cream butter, gradually adding sugar and beat until fluffy; add egg yolks one at a time, continuing to beat until very light and fluffy. Be sure not to underbeat. Add flour along with flavoring and bourbon; fold in stiffly beaten egg whites. Grease a tube pan, line with waxed paper and spread in the bottom a layer of finely chopped pecans. This layer should be about one-fourth inch thick. Carefully pour in batter and bake in moderate over (350 F.) one and one-half hours. Cool in the pan.

SOUR CREAM DEVIL'S FOOD

- ½ cup butter
- 1½ cups brown sugar
- ½ cup sugar
- 2 eggs
- 2 squares chocolate
- ½ cup boiling water
- 1 cup dairy sour cream
- 1 teaspoon soda
- 2 cups cake flour
- 2 teaspoons vanilla
- Chocolate frosting

Cream butter, gradually adding brown and granulated sugars; add eggs and beat thoroughly. Melt chocolate in the boiling water, cool slightly, then stir into the egg mixture. Add the combined soda and flour in about three parts alternately with sour cream. Add vanilla. Stir batter after each addition until it is well blended. Bake in two greased nine-inch layer pans in moderate oven (350 F.) about 25 minutes. Spread with chocolate frosting.

CHOCOLATE FROSTING

- 4 squares chocolate
- ⅓ cup water
- ¾ cup brown sugar
- ¼ cup butter
- 2 egg yolks
- ¼ teaspoon salt
- ¾ teaspoon vanilla
- 2 cups sifted confectioners' sugar

Melt chocolate in water, cook with brown sugar and butter four or five minutes, stirring constantly. Cool. Add egg yolks and salt, beating thoroughly. Add vanilla and add confectioners' sugar until of spreading consistency.

PETITS FOURS

- ½ cup butter
- 1 cup sugar
- 2 eggs
- 2¼ cups flour
- 3 teaspoons baking powder
- ¾ cup milk
- 1 teaspoon vanilla
- Jelly
- Frosting
- Decorations

Cream butter with sugar until light and fluffy; beat in eggs, one at a time. Add flour which has been sifted with baking powder in about three parts, alternating with milk. Add vanilla. Pour in a greased sheet pan, spreading batter about one inch thick. Bake in moderate oven (350 F.) 40 to 45 minutes. Turn out on a cake rack to cool. Split and spread jelly between, then combine and frost. These may be cut into diamonds, squares or rectangles for variation. Decorate each little cake as your fancy dictates, with candied fruits, chopped nuts, or contrasting colored frosting piped through a pastry tube.

Left:
A Hidden Oasis
Behind the triple entrance gates and by the south side of an interior courtyard, a pond is filled with floating heart lilies (*Nymphoides aquaticum*) and framed with vivid geraniums (*Perlargonium hortorum*).

A path of oolitic limestone creates a walkway to the rose garden. Cavendish bananas (*Musa cavendishi*) fill the upper corners. At the top left, an Umbrella tree (*Schefflera actinophylla*) shades the side entry door.

Floating heart is a small water-plant native to South Florida. It was part of the dense primeval growth that filled the deep sloughs of the Everglades. At first glance, floating heart and the other plants in the slough appeared to be of no economic significance, but it is this tangle that makes animal life possible in the Everglades.

Aquatic insect larvae, water snails, and bivalves feed on the floating heart's roots and submerged stems. These creatures become food to small fish. Fish, crustaceans, frogs and surface insects are the meal of larger fish, alligators, snakes, and birds. Dainty floating heart is a poignant reminder of the interconnectedness of all life.

The umbrella tree can grow quite tall, with leaflets in a radial arrangement that is responsible for its nickname, *Schefflera actinophylla*. Showy red inflorescences stand above the foliage and resemble the arms of a gargantuan octopus.

Rear View
The back terrace of the Wolfson home faces a sunset view of Miami's Biscayne Bay. Lounge chairs suggest a moment of relaxation. In the upper reaches of the photo, the concluding arms of the Banyan tree extend skyward.

The Okas

"A hedge of Australia pine
is velvet to the touch,
and guards against intrusion
All over the beach you'll find
this windbreaker
growing in profusion"

Irving Zieman[11]

Australian pines encircle the tropics of the globe. They are wonderfully adapted to Dade County's rocky limestone soil and adept at binding the shifting sand of the shores of the beach when the wind blows. Long lived, they often attain a height of one hundred and fifty feet. Australian pines were brought to Miami Beach as windbreakers for the tropical fruit orchards envisioned on the newly created real estate. These original plantings still exist and can be seen in a double row along Pinetree Drive in Miami Beach.

Early settlers of Dade County carried the easy-growing *Hibiscus* with them, for a cutting planted in the ground flaunted its glorious blossoms in the Florida sun within a year. The hibiscus features a long red projection of pollen-bearing stamen which extends dramatically beyond the perimeter of the petals and terminates in five tiny deep red velvety lobes.

The Oka Family in a formal pose against a hedge of Australian pine *(Casurina equisetifolia)* in the garden of their home, c. 1950. From left to right, Barbara June, Gertrude, Kenneth, Stephanie Heller (in her father's lap) and Michele Lee. Gertrude wears turquoise sandals with a filmy off-the-shoulder gown from Lillie Rubin. The three girls are wearing fine organza dresses with lace bands. A fourth child, Jonathan Kenneth, was born a few years later. Kenneth Oka, lawyer, world traveler, music lover, was to become a judge and twice Mayor of Miami Beach during the glamour-and-growth years linking the 50s and 60s. His passion for music was reflected in his civic life. He was founding President of the Miami Symphony Orchestra, President of the Summer Pops concerts, and President of the Miami Beach Community Concert Series.

"He was not the average politician. He was quite intellectual, very well read. He loved music, literature, poetry. He had a great appreciation for bringing the arts to the city."
Hank Meyer, "Mr. Miami Beach," Miami Beach's greatest publicist[12]

Outdoor photography was de rigueur when this family portrait was taken. After the Oka's home was built in the 1930s, the development of architectural steel and glass allowed architects to open up walls and provide more natural light. Architects abandoned the Mediterranean style to embrace Modernism, and photographers had the option to work indoors.

Previous spreads: Gertrude Oka, c. 1938, holding a cluster of immense *Hibiscus grandiflora,* a pink variety.
Hibiscus photographed by Hans Hannau.

Opposite:
Gertrude leaning against a coconut palm in Lummus Park wearing a playsuit, 1938. A hedge of *Malvaviscus arboreus*, a relative of the hibiscus, is in the background. Stretching the length of Ocean Drive from Sixth Street to 14th Place, Lummus Park was donated to the City in 1912 by the Lummus Brothers's Ocean Beach Realty Company.

A Bermuda grass lawn was immediately planted with the hope that its aggressive root system would supply strong underground runners to hold the sandy soil in place. Coconut palms were planted as well, to provide inviting shade and a sense of site. Finally, a ten foot-wide sidewalk was installed. From 1912 to 1917, the Lummus Brothers spent $40,000 to create and maintain Lummus Park for the people of Miami Beach.

Left:
Barbara June Oka poses by the Shower of Gold *(Cassia fistula)*, late 1940s. Her right arm mimics the smooth barked limb. Joints of movement and growth, the elbow and node are parallel structures.

Healing Plant
The Shower of Gold tree was critical to early people dependent on the properties of nature to heal. *Cassia fistula* was valued by ancient Egyptians for its long cylindrical pods or fruits. Ripening from fresh green in hue to shiny black, these pods grow up to two feet in length. When mature, they contain a sticky brown pulp and several seeds used to cure a multitude of afflictions. Cuttings were carried with the Spanish conquistadors to the New World and firmly planted on the island of Cuba. English naturalist Sir Hans Sloane, practicing medical botany in Jamaica almost three hundred years ago, discussed the curative powers of Cassia and gave a potion for a purgative cure. "The pulp purges twice as much if powdered Seeds be added." Today the medicinal properties of *Cassia fistula* are being rediscovered.[5]

Gertrude Personifies the Era

The 1930s witnessed the development of fashion for sports and leisure, suggesting an entirely new way to dress. The decade of the twenties with its limb-baring fashions had paved the way for less restrictive clothing with higher air-to-skin ratio. Reclining in a languorous pose and wearing a two-piece sun costume, Gertrude personifies the era. A new attitude emanated from the West Coast where, for a brief moment, Hollywood challenged New York as the originator of American style. Women flocked to the movies and absorbed the fashion look of the current beauties. The stars wore bathing suits, and California sportswear manufacturers jumped on the bandwagon to design and market beach clothing.

Discarding thoughts of becoming an actress or chanteuse, Gertrude Heller began teaching Latin at the private Lear School. The school occupied an early mansion built from oolitic limestone on spacious grounds facing Biscayne Bay. The Lear School was filled with children from the North. In those days, doctors prescribed sunny Florida for delicate health and many families found themselves spending cold winter months in warm Miami. Classes were taught outdoors at tables under the trees, leaving the mansion as a retreat for rainy days.

Gertrude Heller with
frangipani in her hair.
The flower was often
her only ornament.

Following spread:
School with Pool
Sunning, studying and
swimming at the
fashionable Lear School,
Miami Beach, 1940.
A year later, Gertrude
ended her career as
a Latin teacher and
married young attorney
Kenneth Oka. The
school brochure must
have become her first
recipe file.

Temple Blossom
The frangipani (Plumeria
acuminata) is native to
tropical America and
one of the tropic's most
fragrant flowers. Only
jasmine can compete
with it in concentration
and sweetness of
scent. Because of this,
the tree is often planted
near temples in the
east, giving frangipani
the association of
sacredness.

The Lear School

BOARDING AND DAY STUDENTS

Mrs. Ida R. Lear, Director

AVENUE · · · MIAMI BEACH, FLORIDA

Detail of front entrance with a fresco design painted by Samuel Heller, Gertrude's father. He was trained in the classical tradition at the Imperial Art Academy in Odessa, Ukraine. For a brief period, Heller painted frescos in convents all over Russia. After emigrating to the United States in the earlier part of the twentieth century, Heller continued to paint frescos in upstate New York.

In later years, Samuel Heller spent weekends copying old master paintings in the Metropolitan Museum of Art in New York, painted frescos in the Metropolitan Opera House, and drew from models at the Art Students League. The walls and furniture of Gertrude Oka's childhood bedroom, as well as the interior of the piano, were transformed by his brush strokes.

The Oka Residence

515 West 30th Street, in Carl Fisher's original Orchard subdivision, was designed in 1934 by pioneer architect Russell T. Pancoast, the architect for many early Miami Beach structures including the Bass Museum of Art. The Oka residence drew on elements from the immensely popular Mediterranean Revival style. Deeply inset front windows gave the house a sense of massiveness. Spanish tiles accented the front entrance, and walls of sun-bleached white stucco were topped with a roof of terra cotta.

Coconut palms flank the front pathway, and giant leafed variegated pothos vines (Rhaphidophora aurea) cling. The pothos is a strong growing vine with a rope-like stem. Large, heart-shaped and shiny leaves are splashed and striped with yellow. The abundant climber is commonly seen growing up the trunks of palms.

The brilliant red, yellow, and green multicolored leaves of the croton (Codiaeum) cluster under the front windows.

A canopy of yellow allamanda (Allamanda cathartica) frames the side window. This sprawling vine with glossy green, whorled leaves and clusters of large, handsome trumpet-shaped flowers has buds as brown as chocolate. The tubes of the flowers are favorite resorts of tree frogs.

Above:
Barbara and Michele Oka, clasping hibiscus blossoms, attired in matching outfits by children's clothing designer Sylvia Whyte, stand in front of a two-toned, white-walled automobile that features the new automatic transmission—a fact written in chrome for the world to see on the side of the car. In the background are clumping date palms and the magnificent royal palms lining Royal Palm Avenue.

Move to Modernism

In 1952, the Okas moved around the corner to Fairgreen Drive to a new split-level home with an open floor plan. Maurice Weintraub is the architect of record, but the concepts of modernism had been absorbed by Gertrude when her sister married Joseph Grunig, a Harvard-trained architect. The new ideal of beauty found in the elimination of the unnecessary was making its debut in Miami Beach. A Florida room, with walls of sliding glass doors, provided uninterrupted views of the outdoors. Cantilevered roof projections, designed to take the place of attached awnings, protected the screened terrace, allowing windows to be left open during ordinary rains.

Following spread:
Florida room featured on partial floor plan of the new Oka residence on Fairgreen Drive.

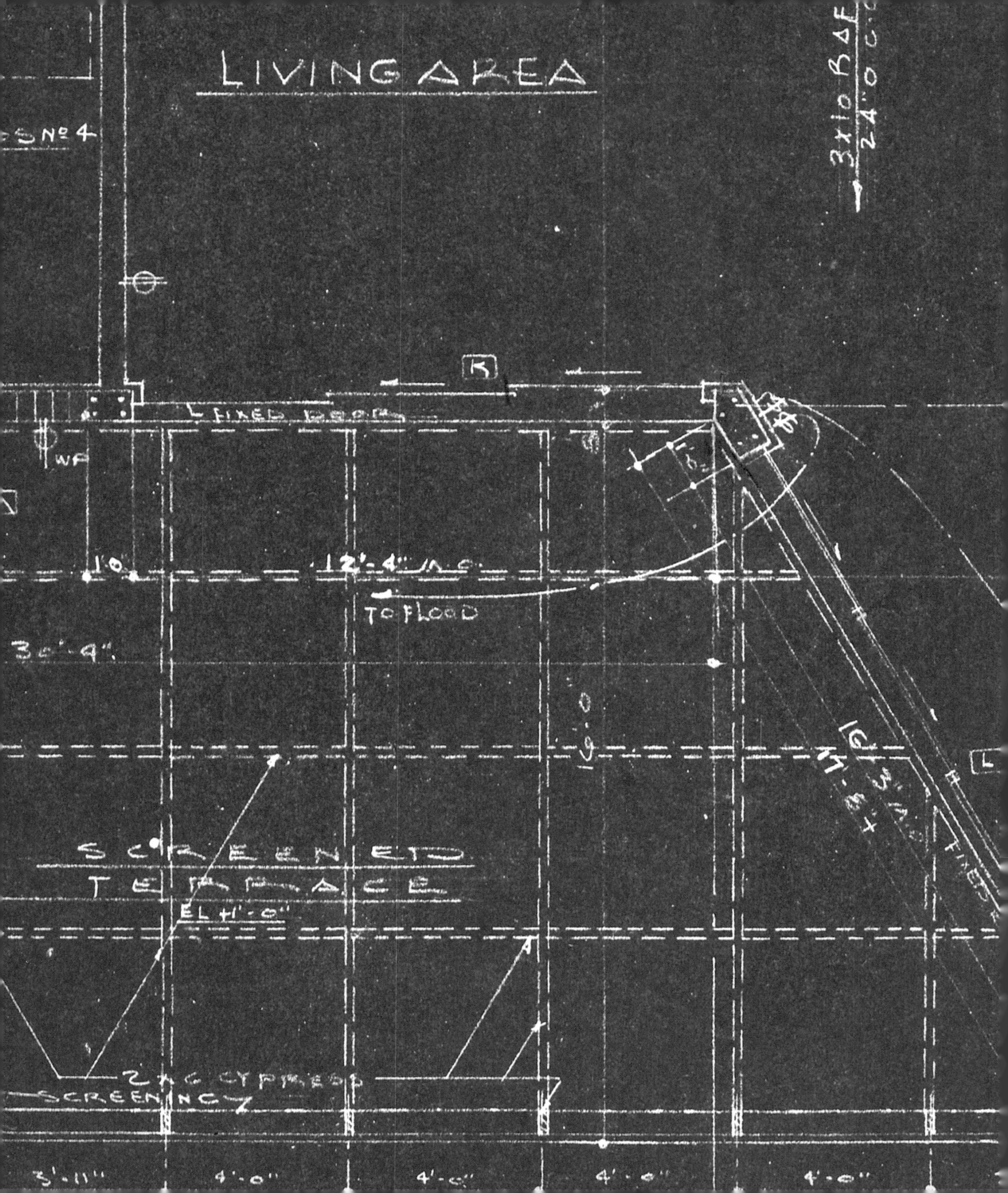

LIVING AREA

3x10 B&F
24.0.C.

FIXED DOOR

WF

R

12'-4" N.G.
TO FLOOD

30'-4"

19'-0"

11'-3" + 10'-3" FIXED

SCREENED
TERRACE
EL +1'-0"

2 x 6 CYPRESS
SCREENING

3'-11"   4'-0"   4'-0"   4'-0"   4'-0"

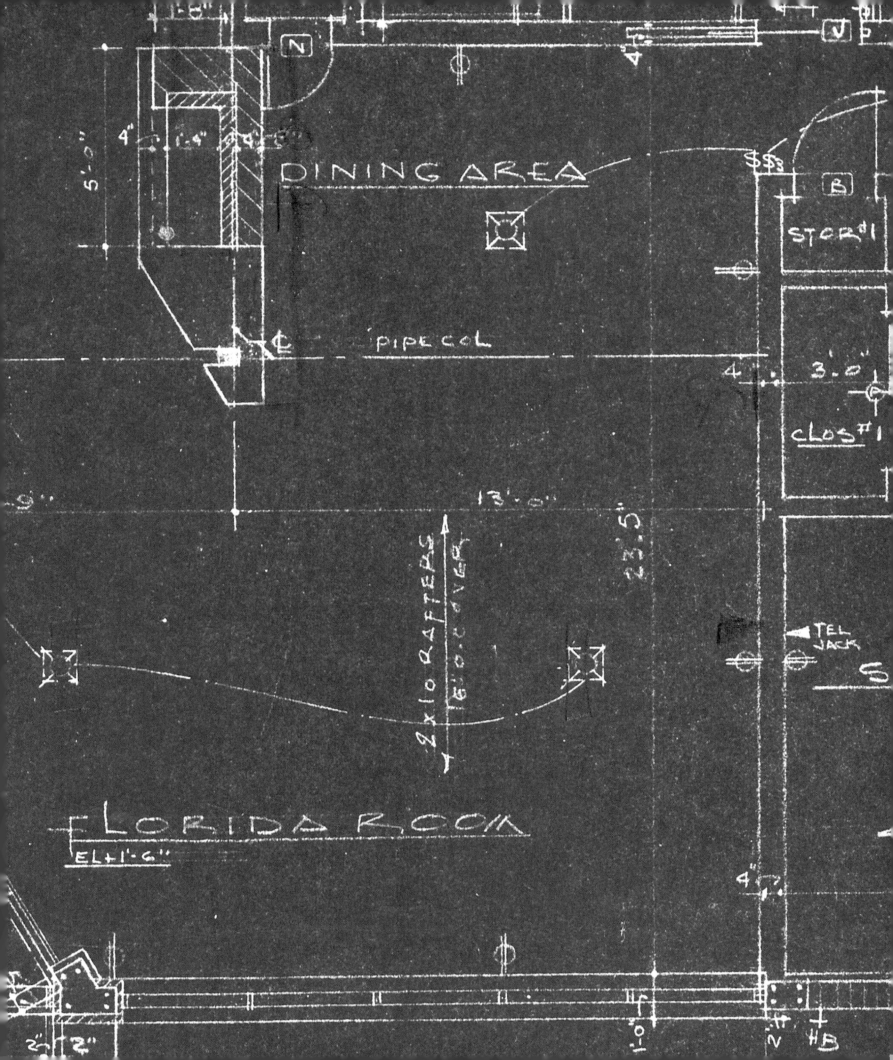

Before Photocopying
The mimeograph
process was patented
by Thomas Edison in
1876, although the
term wasn't used until
his patents were
licensed by Albert
Blake Dick in 1887.
Stencils were created
on waxed tissue paper
using a hand-held
stylus or typewriter.
The completed stencil
was wrapped around
a drum on the
mimeograph machine
and ink was forced
through the marks on
the stencil. The process
was messy.

HOWDY PODNER!

Mrs. Oka

Like Blades of Grass

Marking the sixth grade graduation ceremony for Michele,
Gertrude Oka was guest speaker at a Mother-Daughter
banquet held at North Beach Elementary School in 1957.
Gertrude went to the Miami Beach Public Library and
researched the mother-daughter relationship worldwide.

Several banquets were staged each year, including an
elaborate Thanksgiving Feast celebrated the day before
school closed for vacation. It was catered by the school
cook, known to all as Miss Ruth. Distinguished by her
apple pie, banana bread, and exceptional lunches,
Miss Ruth was summoned from the kitchen several times
each year by Mable Mizner, School Principal, to the
appreciative applause of the children and teachers. The
food was so delicious that Mable Mizner would bring her
friends from the exclusive Surf Club to lunch at the
cafeteria. Miss Ruth would favor them with her famous
iced coffee with vanilla ice cream.

During the 1950s, teaching was the career path most
available to and acceptable for women. A huge pool
of highly intelligent professional women provided the best
possible education to today's baby boomers. [4] Mrs.
Mizner administered an institution where discipline was
countered with creative play.

What Daughters Mean to Mothers

I am very happy this evening to speak to you on the subject of what daughters mean to mothers. Since I have three daughters of my own, I can speak with some authority. However, since the birth of my little son—I can speak about daughters with a much better perspective.

In discussing this subject, it is interesting to note what daughters mean to mothers elsewhere in this world. In the Far East, for example, I remember, as a little girl, I was shocked to see pictures of Chinese women with their feet bound so tightly from early childhood. They could hardly walk. This was symbolic of the bondage of the women of China. This custom is dying out, but there are many other customs that still remain. One of the worst calamities to befall a Chinese woman was the birth of a girl child. The child was regarded as a temporary resident in the household, for as soon as she was married off (at a very early age), her full allegiance was given to her husband, his family, and his ancestors. The lot of the mother was an unhappy one, and that of the child equally so. In such a situation, it was very difficult for a wonderful mother-daughter relationship to exist. Far, far away, in the land of India, the birth of a boy is the great joy of a Hindu mother's life. This places her in the highest and most honorable position in the family. All the relatives bow before her. Is it any wonder that the birth of a daughter is looked upon as a sad event?

However, India is a strange place, filled with many different sects and religions and in that same country—on the western coast—in Malabar—the birth of a girl is the signal for great rejoicing. For here—the women rule the family and tell the men what to do. The children take the mother's name—this is known as a matriarchal society and the laws of inheritance provide that the women must take the greater part of a family's property and wealth. It is reported that the rapport between mother and daughter is a happy and proud one.

Looking back throughout history, it appears to me that the relationship between mother and daughter was greatly dependent on the function and position of the mother in the society of her day. In this country, today's mothers are proud of their daughters—just as much as of their sons. Our daughters are growing up in a society where they are practically on a par with men . . . .

And while they are still ours, growing up in the shelter of our maternal love and protection, there is much that they mean to us and can teach us. In the complexities of day to day living, we sometimes get lost and it takes our daughters to lead us out. They have the power of taking delight in everything and they notice many things we grown ups are apt to miss. With them, we relive our own childhood and experience vicariously the joy of a new party dress, the oohs and ahs over the latest male crooner, the problem of homework, and the awakening interest in so many activities . . .

To conclude I'd like to quote:

"Be patient, oh, be patient! Put your ear against the earth. Listen there how noiselessly the germ o' the seed has birth. How noiselessly and gently it upheaves its little way 'til it parts the scarcely broken ground, And the blade stands up in day."

Our daughters are seeds that noisily and not so gently upheave the scarcely broken ground and like blades of grass reach up into the heavens.

I thank you.

Gertrude Oka
Excerpt from speech, 1957

Miss Ruth's
Banana Bread

1/2 cup shortening
1 cup sugar
2 eggs
3 ripe bananas (mashed)
2 cups flour
1/2 tsp. salt
1 tsp. baking soda
1 cup chopped nuts
1/2 tsp. vanilla

Cream shortening and sugar. Add bananas. Sift dry ingredients and add. Lastly add nuts and vanilla.

Bake in 350 degree oven in a loaf pan for one hour or until cake tester comes out dry.

Portrait of Kenneth Oka for his first of many political races, Justice of the Peace for Miami Beach. Photo: Arnold Newman

Opposite:
Portrait of Barbara June Oka, 1945. Published in the Miami Beach *Sun Tropic*, the Future Belle of the Beach was wearing a fine damask cotton striped dress with scattered bouquets of roses. The caption for the photograph included the Oka's home address— the world, at least in Miami Beach, was considered a safe place. Photo: Arnold Newman

Running for Election

In 1941 photographer Arnold Newman and fledgling attorney Kenneth Oka both had offices in the Albion Hotel on Lincoln Road. Oka had just returned to Miami Beach from Harvard University, where he completed his education in law. When he needed a press photograph for his first campaign for Justice of the Peace, he went next door to the Newman Studio. Oka had not yet discarded the wardrobe of the northern climate; his choice of jacket for this initial career gesture is a not-very-tropical wool herringbone tweed. The Miami *Herald* published this photograph to announce Oka's candidacy.

Arnold Newman in Miami Beach

Born in New York City, Arnold Newman and his family arrived in Miami Beach in 1934. He was educated at Miami Beach High School and studied art at the University of Miami. He left soon after and returned to New York City, where he had his first exhibition at the A.D. Gallery in 1941. His work was mostly portraiture, developing an approach that is considered widely influential in portrait photography today. Increasingly important exhibits, purchases and commissions followed until World War II brought Newman back to Miami Beach awaiting a draft call that never came. In the meantime he documented some of the people, places, and natural occurrences of Florida in a rather abstract style. When he took the portraits of Kenneth Oka and Barbara June Oka, he had already captured Piet Mondrian with his camera and had traded Mondrian a portrait of the artist for the preliminary drawing for "Boogie Woogie Broadway."[15]

Miami Beach of the Orient

Mayor Kenneth Oka fostered Miami Beach's participation in President Eisenhower's newly-minted People to People Program and instituted the city affiliation between Miami Beach and Fujisawa, Japan. This bond gained national and international publicity for Miami Beach.

In recognition for his outstanding work in foreign relations, Oka received the annual People to People Award in New York City from United Nations Ambassador James Wadsworth. Gertrude took up the brush while spending several months visiting all of her new Japanese friends in the "Miami Beach of the Orient."

Ink drawing by Gertrude Oka, c. 1960

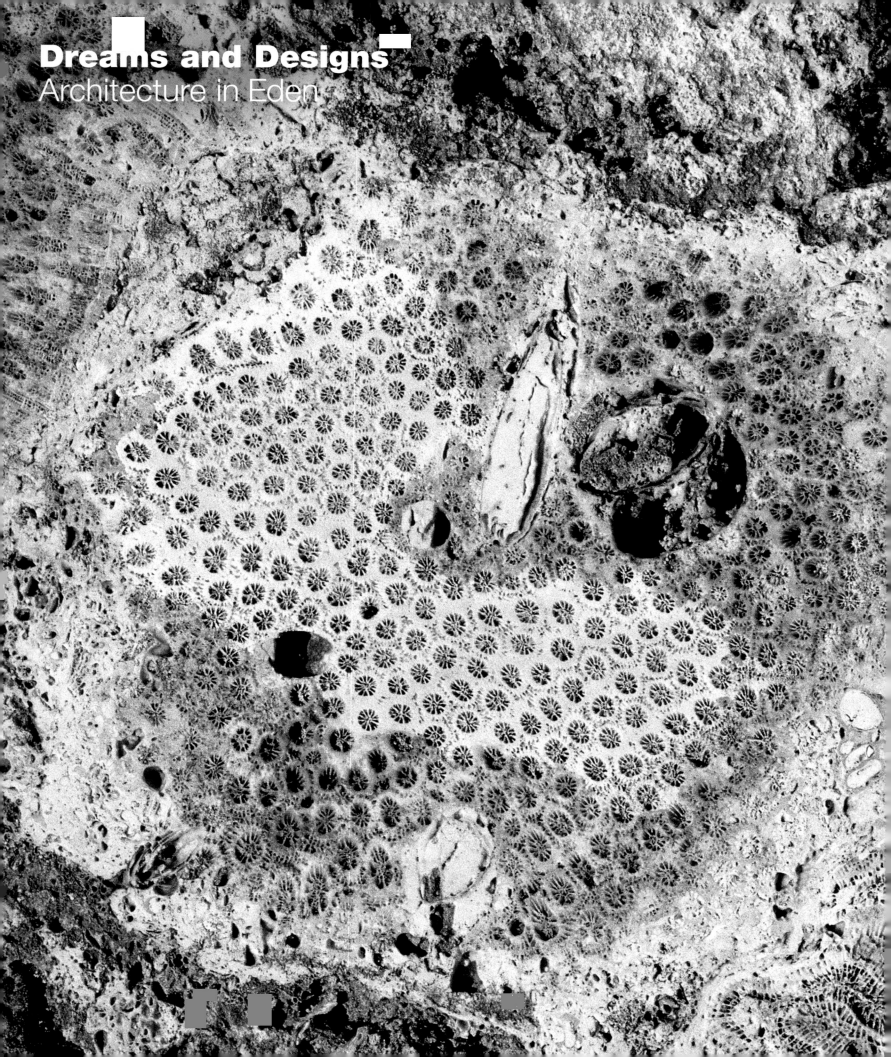

Dreams and Designs
Architecture in Eden

Previous spread:
An ancient compost
heap, Miami oolitic
limestone from
the facade of the Bass
Museum. Note the
brain coral, starlet coral
(Siderastrea) and the
residue of mollusk
shells. The crevices
seduce the eye and are
characteristic of the
way rainwater
works on oolitic stone,
creating unusual
shapes and forms as
it tunnels through the
intricate structure.

THE WOLFSON INITIATIVE CORPORATION

2399 Northeast Second Avenue
Miami, Florida 33137
(305) 573-0444
Telex: 5101011331

Dear Michele,

The land we stand on was in fact deliberately created to accommodate buildings. Miami Beach was then, as it is now, a land development project from which the founding fathers intended to make money. But the architecture, of whatever style or period, was always imported. This makes one wonder what kind of identifiable architecture could ever characterize a manufactured landscape in the first place.

What kind of people would choose to inhabit an invented landscape brought in on barges and architecture delivered in boxcars? The answer, I believe, is either people captivated by possibility or people who, finding themselves here, simply proceeded to exploit the set for whatever it might turn out to be worth. Still, in the long run this appropriated architecture eventually became "native" by serving as the looking glass of immigrant aspirations. Visually effective but shoddily crafted buildings of the '30s and '40s soon became objects of ridicule. But their gratuitous ornamentation and their modest claims on time, place, and climate tended to bolster the morale of the survivors of the Depression. Today they stand as authentic examples of what we now accept as the legacy of Miami Beach.

In a paradise of the prodigal where all rules were meant to be broken, architecture then became a matter of largely whimsical contrivance in the service of expropriation. Then you and I and all of us became the uncritical heirs of the grand gesture. From the Roney Plaza to the Fontainebleau. A grand gesture, but to what? Looking back, what excited us was ostentation, pure and simple. The super-abundant baroque of post-war structures in the '50s would become even more eclectic celebrations of prosperity. Or, if you like, the homegrown happenings of the era of Eisenhower.

Michele, let's do a tour of the past and revisit the sites of our shared architectural autobiography. In other words, we'll conjure up those structures that our families inhabited and in which our memories dwell. Points of interest, a chronological field guide to habitations, shrines, and institutions.

Micky

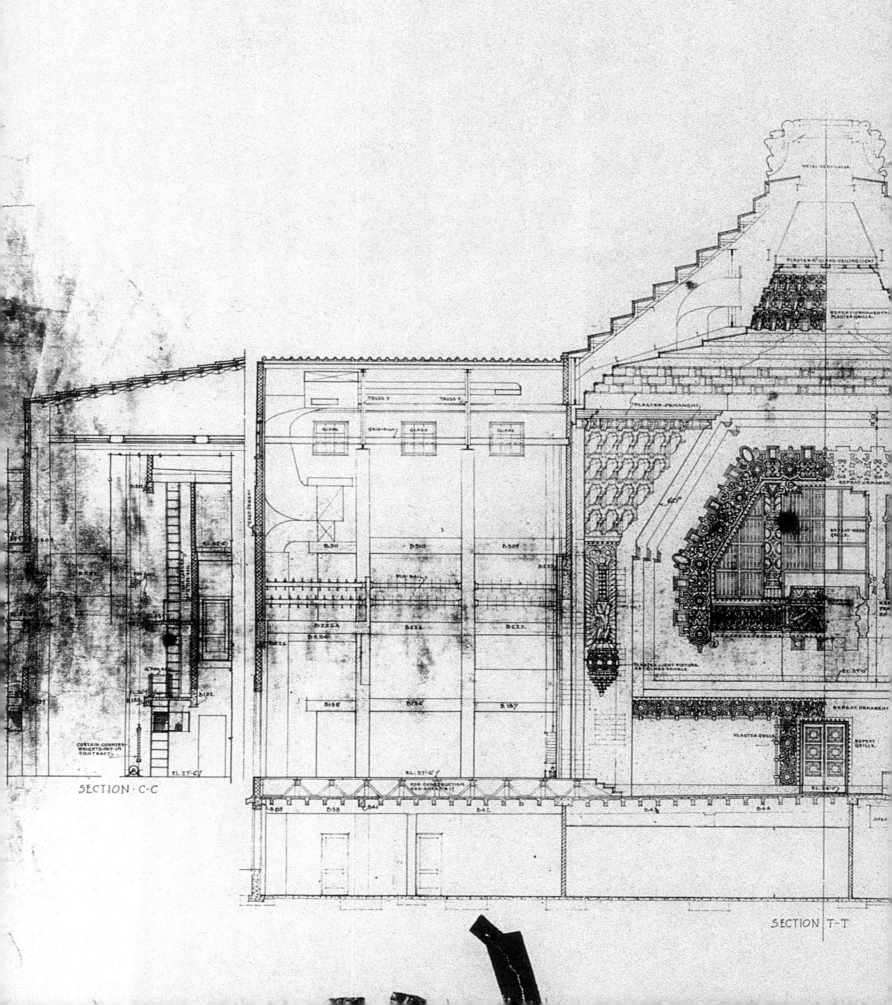

SECTION·C-C

SECTION T-T

Aztec Revival Meets Miami River

The Scottish Rite Masonic Temple, half a million square feet of poured concrete, was built by Kiehnel and Elliott in 1917. The Pittsburgh firm had been brought to Miami to build El Jardin, the winter home of John Bindley, President of the Pittsburgh Steel Company.

The energy of the boom was perceptible, and Richard Kiehnel stayed to open a Miami office. Born in Germany, Kiehnel studied at Ecole des Beaux-Arts in Paris, a school credited with greatly influencing American architecture of the early twentieth century.

The pyramidal Scottish Rite Masonic Temple is perfumed by the exotic scent of Egyptian Revival that was popular in Europe during Kiehnel's formative student years. Kiehnel became known for great evocative gestures. Fifty hand-painted Biblical scenes adorn the Temple walls. After building the Scottish Rite Masonic Temple, Kiehnel went on to become a major force in developing Miami's Mediterranean architecture.

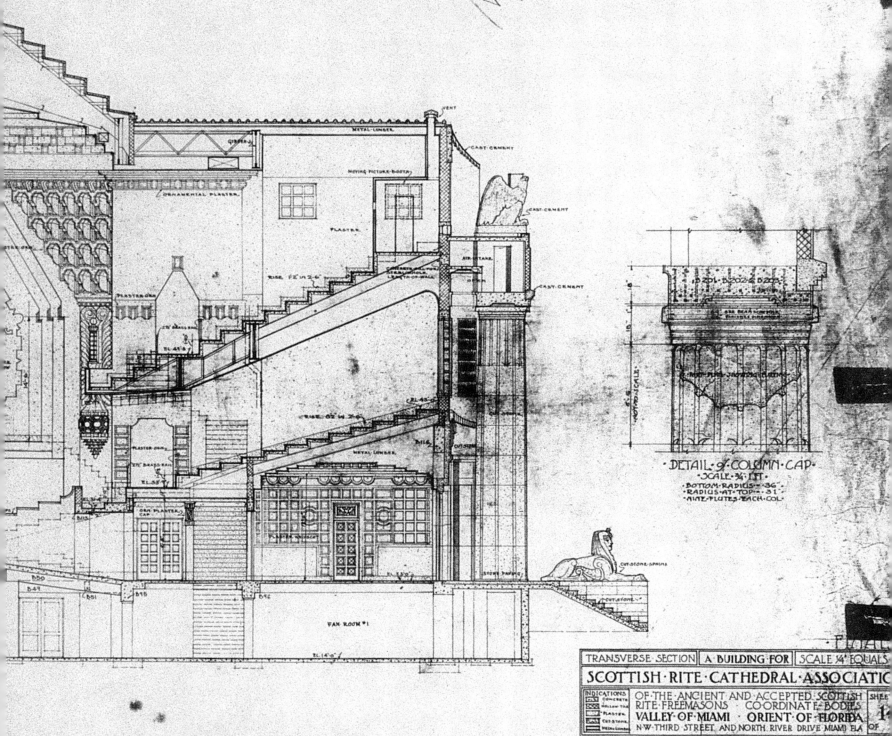

· DETAIL · OF · COLUMN · CAP ·
· SCALE · ¾" = 1 FT ·
· BOTTOM · RADIUS · 36 ·
· RADIUS · AT · TOP · 31 ·
· NINE · FLUTES · EACH · COL ·

TRANSVERSE · SECTION | A · BUILDING · FOR | SCALE ¼" EQUALS
SCOTTISH · RITE · CATHEDRAL · ASSOCIATION
OF · THE · ANCIENT · AND · ACCEPTED · SCOTTISH
RITE · FREEMASONS · CO-ORDINATE · BODIES
VALLEY · OF · MIAMI · ORIENT · OF · FLORIDA
N.W. THIRD STREET AND NORTH RIVER DRIVE MIAMI FLA

KIEHNEL · AND · ELLIOTT · ARCHITECTS
PITTSBURGH · PA · AND

Detail of a Florida orange tree early in its yearly cycle—blossom, small green fruit, and ripeness.

Opposite:
Frances Louise Cohen Wolfson

Clusters of Orange Blossoms

The Scottish Rite Masonic Temple was the scene of the wedding of Miss Frances Louise Cohen to Mitchell Wolfson. Gladiolus, ferns, and white lady slippers combined with potted palms to set the stage for the ceremony. Mrs. Herbert Fiebleman sang "Indian Love Call." Frances wore a gown of white Georgette heavy with embroidered crystals. A court train of silver cloth was attached to the shoulders of her dress. A veil was held in place by a coronet of pearls embroidered on a piece of lace from the wedding dress of the bride's mother. Clusters of orange blossoms were caught at either side of the head piece, and also trimmed the bottom of the veil.[1]

The Neptune

The Neptune, an apartment building at 1632 Meridian Avenue at Lincoln Road, was designed by architect J.C. Gault in 1925. This early structure is considered a good example of ornamented Mediterranean revival. The exterior patio entrance is accented by square pedestals supporting classical urns. The entrance to the building is flanked by a pair of Corinthian pilasters with detailed pediments. The stucco exterior contains scrolls, a crest, and a finial on the rooftop. Balconies provide exterior space for some of the thirty-five units. A momentary player in the great boom era, J. C. Gault built seven structures during a single year in Miami Beach, including The Flagler Federal Savings Bank. Purchased by Sam Oka in 1936, the Neptune was the first of several properties acquired by the Oka family. As we can read on the card below, the family was off to a great start in their real estate ventures in south Florida. The building remained in the family until 2004.

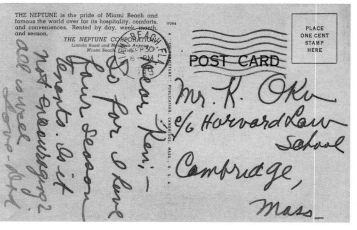

Fronting the Neptune was a shrub commonly referred to as the copper-leaf (Acalypha wilkesiana). The colors of the leaves can be variegated: green, red, maroon, pink, or entirely red or rich copper, from which the plant derives its name. Variations of tone and color are responsible for the copper-leaf's also being referred to as the biblical "Jacob's Coat."

The leaves are large, up to eight inches, soft, heart-shaped and tooth-edged. Its catkins, in contrast, are red short spikes. Commonly used in early foundation plantings, the copper-leaf is returning to today's landscaped gardens.

Right:
Lincoln Road before Shopping
Lincoln Road at James Avenue, c.1918. A protective iron fence, one most likely dismantled for the war effort, surrounds a young Ficus microcarpa. Pandanus baptisti, a low spreading variegated cluster forming magnificent clumps, is in the foreground.

North Beach Elementary School

Blueprint detailing
the entrance, 1935

Next spread:
PWA photograph, 1936

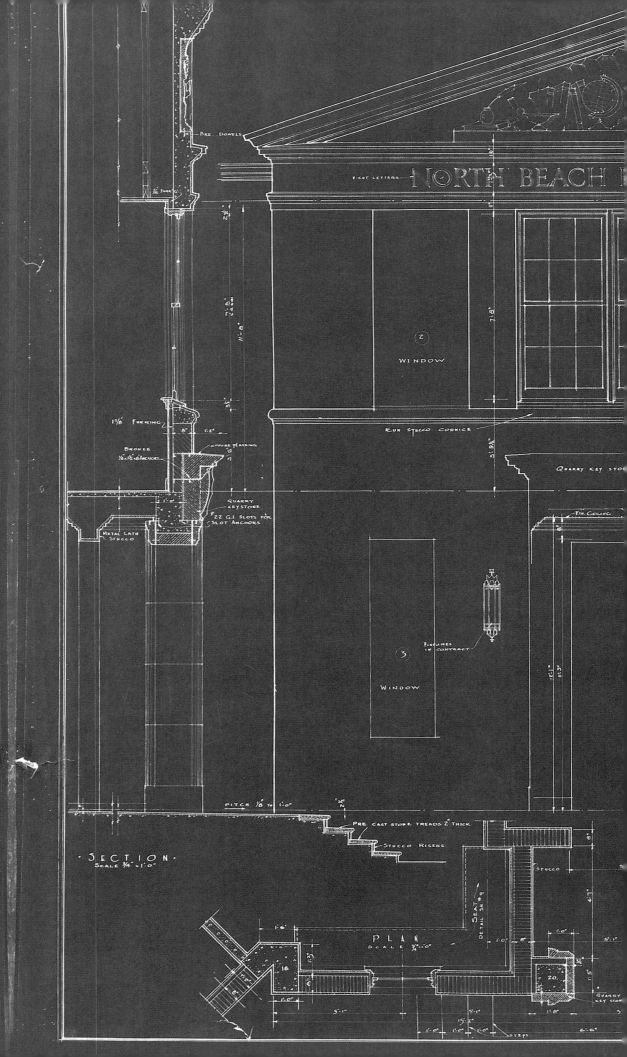

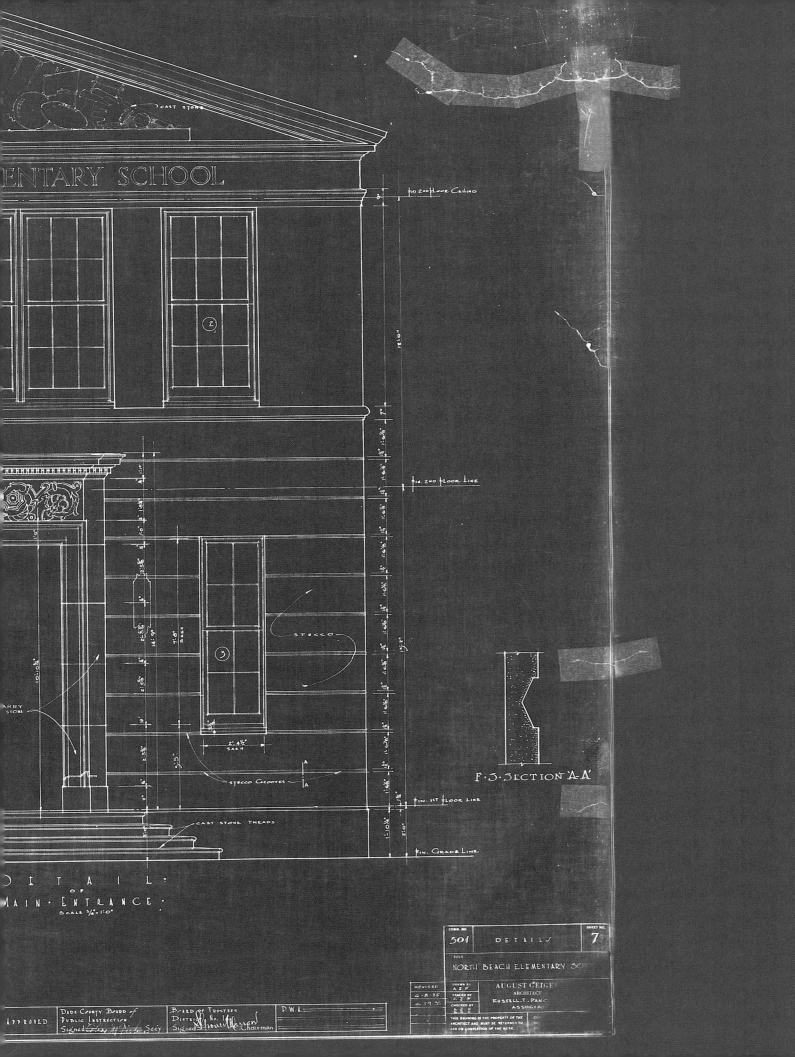

ENTARY SCHOOL

CAST STONE

2nd Floor Ceiling

Fin. 2nd Floor Line

STUCCO

STUCCO GROOVES

CAST STONE TREADS

Fin. 1st Floor Line

Fin. Grade Line

DETAIL
OF
MAIN · ENTRANCE ·
SCALE 3/4" = 1'·0"

F·S·SECTION 'A-A'

COMM. NO.	DETAILS	SHEET NO.
501		7

TITLE
NORTH BEACH ELEMENTARY SCHOOL

REVISED	DRAWN BY A.J.F.	AUGUST GEIGER
6-8-36	TRACED BY A.J.F.	ARCHITECT
4-29-36	CHECKED BY A.J.F.	RUSSELL.T.PANCOAST
		ASSOCIATE

THIS DRAWING IS THE PROPERTY OF THE
ARCHITECT AND MUST BE RETURNED TO
HIM ON COMPLETION OF THE WORK.

"Architecture like all art is never static but is undergoing a continual process of change. The change is due not only to the development of new needs, new materials, and new methods of construction but also to the desire, inherent in successive generations of man, to produce something better and different from that accomplished by the preceding generations, something which will outlast the short span of a lifetime and will remain as monuments for the generations to come."

Tropical School

North Beach Elementary School, commissioned by the Public Works Administration (PWA), was designed by August Geiger and Russell T. Pancoast in 1936. A bronze plaque at the entrance of North Beach Elementary reads "Federal Emergency Administration of Public Works Portion of Project, No. 8214, 1936." Located on the Northwest corner of 41st Street and Meridian Avenue, NBES occupied the site of a former dairy farm and contained a row of barns for horses from nearby Polo Park.

In 1914, architect August Geiger wrote a seminal article, "The Model School Plan for Tropic Florida," reinventing the environment where children were to remain for the greater part of a day. He discarded the model typical of northern practice, a square or rectangular building permitting no cross-ventilation. Geiger substituted elongated covered loggias for interior halls and kept the buildings one room deep. Thus he achieved his goal of sunlight and a free flow of air in all classrooms. Geiger thought like an artist. His palette was sun mixed with tints of South Florida. He imagined that the red tiled roof, the rough stucco walls of cream over the concrete construction, and the omnipresent blue sky characteristic of the Miami area to be a cheerful combination. The native rock, oolitic limestone, carved into a foliant motif, was incorporated into the facade as a special touch.

The PWA built North Beach Elementary School for two reasons. It was committed, first of all, to increasing employment in both the building industries and in factories which supplied building materials during the years of depression. Second, there was already a sense of the more complex future ahead. The concept of elementary education was expanding to include the exploration of the sciences, arts, music, nature study, shop, dramatics, and even physical education. The new school buildings were to provide the structure for this richer, more varied educational experience. When North Beach Elementary School was built, it contained twelve classrooms, a clinic, two offices, a cafeteria and physical education room. Two stories in height, it took a year to complete and cost $127,000. A substantial auditorium was soon added, and quickly became the focal point for the school community. North Beach Elementary School educated well the children from the Pancoast, Tashiro, Wolfson, and Oka families, and continues an ambitious humanistic mandate today.

Opposite:
"The Orange Blossom Song" was sung at North Beach Elementary School and by school children all over the state of Florida until the 1960s. A true folk song, it was passed along by music teachers on hand written sheet music or by the human voice.

The ending varied from region to region. The version sung at North Beach included one variant ending:
"I want to wander through the orange groves where the children used to roam, Oh take me back to Florida, it's the place I call my home."

When standardized sheet music was introduced in Florida schools in the sixties, "The Orange Blossom Song" disappeared from the classroom.

Orange Blossom Song

Mayors

Mayor Mitchell Wolfson at the desk, top floor, City Hall, 1943. Wolfson served briefly in 1943, prior to departing for active combat in World War II.

Mayor Kenneth Oka at the desk, top floor, City Hall. Oka served two terms, 1957 to 1959 and 1961 to 1963.

Opposite:
Miami Beach City Hall at 1130 Washington Avenue, designed by Martin L. Hampton, 1927 to 1928, was the site of the mayor's offices.

Deco Lincoln Road
Appropriating the form of an ocean liner at sea, the Albion was designed by Igor B. Polevitzky and T. Russell in 1939.

99

World renowned
photographer Arnold
Newman in his studio
darkroom at the Albion,
September, 1943.
During his short tenure
at the Albion, Newman
photographed "Studio
Light, 1944," a dramatic
still life published
decades later in *Arnold
Newman in Florida*.

Inside the Albion

Sited on a prominent corner, the intersection of James
and Lincoln Road, the Albion had a pool with a garden
deck popular with the young crowd, peep-hole portholes
for viewing legs underwater, and a fabulous soda fountain,
The Fountain Blue, which was nicknamed the "home of
the overflowing soda." The Albion extended into office
spaces that fronted fashionable Lincoln Road. The street
level consisted of retail shops which catered to the needs
and pleasures of sun seekers. The Albion Beauty Salon,
with practitioner Lela Wielt, remained open until 10:00 in
the evening. On the upper level, professionals—doctors,
lawyers, dentists, and photographer Arnold Newman—
rented office spaces.

Thrifty Design

The interiors of the cocktail lounge and The Baroque Room at the Albion were executed in 1946 by Paul Silverthorne. He constructed the fantasy of this room during the postwar years when a shortage of materials, government restrictions, and new fire code statutes could have been an obstacle course. Silverthorne jumped the hurdles, using plaster of Paris and a coat of paint.

The fabulous Baroque Room at the Albion, a plaster of Paris fantasy

The RONEY PLAZA
MIAMI BEACH

Open All Year

At twenty-third is the Plaza called the Roney,
Named for the builder who ran away with all the money.
It was built in twenty-five when the country was on a fling.
While our silent president was saving pieces of string.
Among the oldest and largest hotels it has no peer:
It faces new competition with a hint of fear,
The secret?

The building hasn't taken all the land;
It left enough for a garden, a paradise on sand
With circular fountains dancing like ballerinas as one,
Where soloist and cherub gaily spout in harmonious tone.
A putting green for recreation
Is enhanced by tropical vegetation.
An oval pond where white ducks come and go
Is the only thing around resembling snow.
The ocean front is seven hundred feet,
Is that a waste of space?

Well—it's a treat!

Irving Zieman[2]

The Roney Plaza
Hotel, a pink confection
that dominated the
Miami Beach skyline
from 1926 to 1966.

102

Fantasy, Luxury,
First Cabañas

The fabulous Roney Plaza, at 23rd and Collins Avenue, was built at the height of the first Florida boom in 1925-26 by the New York firm of Schultze and Weaver at a cost of $2 million.[3] This huge pink oceanfront resort was the first to introduce and market the cabaña concept. The Roney Plaza towered into the sky, well past the tree line, and was visible from all over Miami Beach. At night its lights provided a scene of enchantment against the starry sky. The Roney was frequented by celebrity visitors and local families. It provided everyone with the ingredients that still make a resort great today: fantasy, luxury, and a front row seat from which to observe the grandeur of nature.

Demolished in 1968 after a short life span of only four decades, the Roney Plaza remains a symbolic landmark for residents of Miami Beach who still recall her charm. In 1928, Schultze and Weaver erected the luxurious and romantic Pierre Hotel on Fifth Avenue in New York City, and went on to build the world-renowned Waldorf-Astoria Hotel in the Art Deco style on Park Avenue in 1931.

Gertrude at the Roney Cabaña Club with Barbara June, July 1945.

Right:
A five-year-old Barbara June Oka in the Roney Plaza garden. She models an Alice in Wonderland plaid apron dress with a hoop skirt underneath by designer Ruth Throne for Sylvia Whyte. Lincoln Road, January 4, 1948. The famous cherub fountain was carved from oolitic limestone. Bougainvillea (*Bougainvillea glabra*) cover the ground in a frame of exuberant hues.

Runway at The Roney

The outdoor fashion show was a popular form of entertainment for visitors, residents, and prospective buyers as well. Miami's Fashion Council sponsored two major fashion shows each year, and the Roney Plaza, with its large and luxurious garden, was a popular site. Runways were constructed under the palms for models to exhibit the new styles for designers and manufacturers of children's and women's clothing. Buyers from all over the United States as well as Latin America attended and placed their purchasing orders. Note the many uniformed men and women in this photograph from the World War II era.

The Shore Club

Opposite:
The Cromwell Hotel

The pineapple is a symbol of tropical regions around the world. The Florida pineapple industry began in 1860 with slips from Havana brought from the Keys. Cuban slips were considered superior in both size and the actual stock. The Cuban planting system, imported as well, set plants ten inches apart in double rows, saving hard labor. In 1890 there was a famous east coast pineapple belt from Fort Pierce south to Miami which eventually succumbed to freezing weather. John Collins attempted to reestablish pineapple plantations as one of the crops in his new tropical paradise, but Miami Beach soil was too light and sandy to sustain the pineapple's growth, for pineapples need humus. The pineapple served at the Shore Club was most likely imported from the West Indies, for airplane travel was not as readily available in the 1950s and Hawaiian pineapple was still arriving at our shore in cans on boats.

The Cromwell and the Shore Club

Built in 1939 for developer N.B.T. Roney by architect Robert A. Taylor, the Cromwell hotel provided additional space for a rapidly growing Miami Beach resort. Gone is the plaster gingerbread of the Roney Plaza and the applied stucco designs of Mediterranean architectural appropriation. Instead, a stark white cube in the modernist tradition makes an appearance. Even the umbrellas surrounding the pool at the Cromwell were white.

Next door at the Shore Club, the bright colors of the Caribbean dominated in the canvas awnings of the cabañas and umbrellas crowning the pool side tables. Palms provided shade for the clientele on the hottest days, and pineapple à la mode was the favored pool side snack. Everything swayed in the ocean breezes, even the fringes of the umbrellas and the fronds of the coconut palms.

Master of Ceremonies

Smitty at the Shore Club with Louis Wolfson II. Smitty, and other fitness buffs like him, were "the entertainment" provided by cabaña clubs during the 1940s. Hired to host and supervise, they exuded physical strength and personal charm, and played with the children, usually offering rudimentary gymnastics. They served as unofficial masters of ceremony at the pools. The structure in the background on the right was Hans Hannau's office and studio for more than ten years.

Father of the Modern Postcard

Viennese photographer Hans Hannau worked at the Cromwell Hotel and the Shore Club, photographing guests for $5 per picture. He arrived in Miami Beach in 1940 and rented a cabaña as his studio. When a teen-aged Grace Kelly and her Philadelphia family visited, Grace was photographed by Mr. Hannau. The results were included in her portfolio when she went to New York in pursuit of an acting career. Hannau is self-described as the father of the modern postcard. During the decade that he photographed at the Cromwell, an influx of soldiers and tourists, all wanting to send home a postcard, converged on the hotel. Their demand resulted in greater product awareness. Hannau's contribution to the modern postcard was a refinement of the existing system: he produced superior photographic images and then demanded the best printing methods from postcard publishers. He also expanded the "cheesecake" genre with photographs of pretty girls in tight bathing suits. These were especially popular during the war years and helped establish his long career in picture postcards.[4]

Bathing Beauty
Marlene Schmidt, Miss Universe 1961. Press opportunities abound at the Fontainebleau beach as the new Miss Universe takes to her job as a duck to water. What could be more quintessentially Miami Beach than a bathing beauty in a white swimsuit hugging a beach ball and posing in front of a striped umbrella? The blond, the ball, and the stretched canvas are a recipe for fun.

Flowers and Fashion

Gertrude Oka hosts a tea and fashion show by Gilda's Boutique at the Shelborne Hotel in honor of Mrs. Bice de Benedictis (mother-in-law of the Costa Rican President), right, and Miss Ileana Lara (niece of the Costa Rican President), left, 1962.

Twenty Latin American women from three Central American countries—Costa Rica, El Salvador, and Nicaragua—attend a series of events that coincide with the opening of the $200,000 garden center and conservatory on a five acre site backing onto the old Collins Canal. In other years, these stylish representatives of Caribbean garden clubs had visited Miami on garden tours.

Gertrude is dressed in black linen with white organza trim and hand-beaded floral appliqués. The dramatic neckline worn by the President's niece sets off her neck and face and extraordinary hat. Señora de Benedictis is elegantly turned out in a velvet hat and studded pectoral neckline.

It seems that there was a consensus on what constituted a stylish woman in the realm of Latin culture. Not tailored New York chic or California movie style. For Gertrude, this Latin style was a conscious adaptation of the region and came as naturally to her as speaking Spanish.

Opposite:
The Modernist Shelborne

Just south of the Cromwell and Shore Club, the Shelborne was built in 1941 by Igor B. Polevitzky, "a little-known giant of Modern architecture."[5] Polevitzky had completed the Albion two years previously. While the Albion was streamlined modernism, the Shelborne clearly reached into the future and became one of the Beach's first buildings to embrace the new International style.

Note the graphics from this photograph taken in the early 1940s. A major alteration of signage took place in the 1950s and has remained for the last five decades. The Shelborne had an impressive lobby with up-to-the-minute comfortable seating arrangements. It hosted visiting dignitaries to the city of Miami Beach from all over the world.

Fontainebleau by the Ocean

The first hotel designed by infamous architect Morris Lapidus, the Fontainebleau was an architectural showcase. Lapidus had previously designed store interiors. Built in 1954, the hotel cost $14 million and occupied a generous site on Collins Avenue at 44th Street, where Collins Avenue jogs back one block from the ocean. The location was formerly the estate of Harvey Firestone, Firestone Tires, Akron, Ohio.

The Fontainebleau provided a backdrop for the stars and wannabes that flocked to join the rich and the famous. The hotel linked Hollywood and Miami Beach, and even shop girls dressed like their favorite actresses. During the peak years of Miami Beach as a magnet for the greater world, the hotel was the site of Miss Universe events, the annual Mayor's conference, Symphony Club balls and a multitude of other glamorous events. The local residents booked their Sweet Sixteen parties, senior proms, and weddings. The Oka family leased Fontainebleau cabañas for a decade of summers, and savored the giant ice cream sodas in the Chez Bon Bon Coffee Shop. The coffee shop lived up to its name: good good.

Postcard of the newly opened Fontainebleau, Miami Beach, 1954, signed by photographer Hans Hannau.

Royalty at the Fontainebleau

Dinner at the first Symphony Club Ball, the Soirée Symphonique, January 1955, was attended by, left to right, Empress Soroya, General James Van Fleet, and the Shah of Iran. Other guests included four security guards, John Astor, and Baron and Baroness Stackelberg.

Mrs. Mitchell Wolfson, President of the Symphony Club, was delighted that the ball was such a brilliant success. More than 600 guests from greater Miami attended. To top off the evening, the entire University of Miami Symphony Orchestra played selections at midnight. It was reported that Queen Soroya's long earrings of rubies and diamonds glittered in the lights. She was noted to be extremely shy and not one to smile very often.

"We may be wrong, but we think that this is the first time reigning royalty has graced a party in Miami. . . . And what a party it was! The new and elegant Fontainebleau provided an out-of-this-world setting."
The Miami *Herald*, January 17, 1955[6]

Shadows of War

To my sweetheart and wife.

This is a copy of my letter to the children. You know my love for you - we were real sweethearts. Keep your chin up! I know you will raise the children as I wanted. Five, sturdy citizens. You are my love.

September 1, 1943

Mitchell.

To my son, Louis Wolfson,
to my son, Mitchell Wolfson Jr., and
to my daughter, Frances Louise Wolfson.

I am addressing this letter to you, my dear children, because if something should happen to me, I want to leave a message for you, which I hope you will carry in your heart and in your conscience all your lives.

I have tried to be a good father to you, and believe that while I have provided materially for you, it is really of no great importance whether I have provided too much, somewhat too little, or moderately. I do believe however, that my financial arrangements will secure for all of you, a good education, also that you will not be in need or lack of food and comfortable housing, especially if you are moderate in your needs, and careful with your expenditures.

I recommend that you keep our theatre business, or rather keep your interest in the business, and try to develop it for the benefit of the public, of your employees, and of you and your families.

I was very happy and proud to be granted the opportunity to serve our country. All of us should thank God every night that we have a country to serve. I only hope and pray that all of you will have the same opportunities and privileges that your mother, I, and all free americans have had for so many years.

My supreme sacrifice, if it should be, is to set an example for you, so that you may always prove worthy of your obligations and duties, and it will not be in vain, if you make of yourselves a credit to our people, as I have always tried to do.

We have always conducted our business in an ethical manner with the thought uppermost in my mind that "He profits most who serves best."

Also we have never invested in or leased any real estate of ours to liquor establishments, gambling establishments, or pawn brokers. Grandfather Wolfson established this custom. I continued it, and I hope you will.

I have no objection to people who care to engage in this business, but I do not believe the profits from this business could ever morally justify your engaging directly or indirectly in this type of business.

Be fair to your employees, associates and to the public. Insist on what is just and right for yourselves, but also grant the same justice to others.

120

Dear Michele,

What a fabulous celebration is architecture--the
concretization of the imagination. And that's one ingredient
pre-war Miami had in abundance. And then came World War II.
The battle lines were drawn--the curtain falls on Eden. The
reality of U boat attacks just off the beach, the enormous
influx of military personnel, the transformation of a
playground to barracks with recreational facilities was
pretty dramatic. I don't remember that final parting with the
future Colonel as he marched off to war. Too young, being
born in 1939, but I read later that his resignation from City
Hall and his volunteering for the Army caused quite a stir
within the family and without. But off he went to return
victorious three years later. I remember that I must have
given him the benefit of the doubt (as to his paternity) for
I greeted the startled conquering hero with, "they told me
who you are and I guess I'll get used to you." Poor man. He
always had a rough time with his youngest. Do you remember
what happened? When? What about Ken? Didn't he join the Coast
Guard and help defend the home front?

Micky

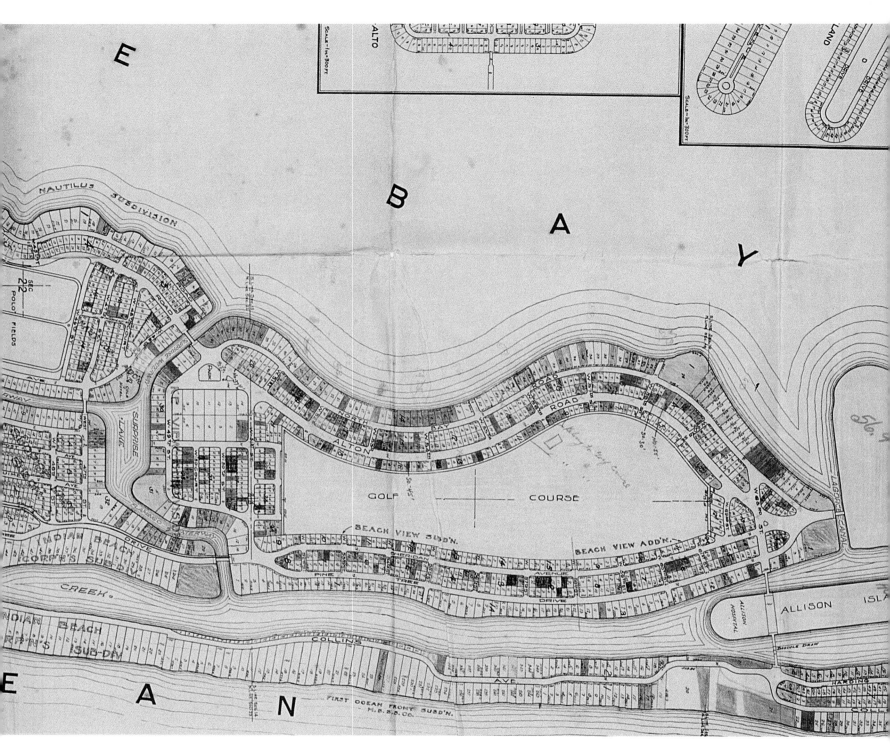

Strategic Maps

Both of these strategic
maps attained their
goals. The plats on the
Miami Beach map are
occupied today and the
final offensive plotted
by the Sixth Army was
triumphant.

Above:
Miami Beach Map,
c. 1920, illuminates the
strategy of real estate
speculators with a
system based on color:
red indicated inventory,
blue detailed property
claimed, and green
sited foreclosures. An
"X" denoted an existing
structure.

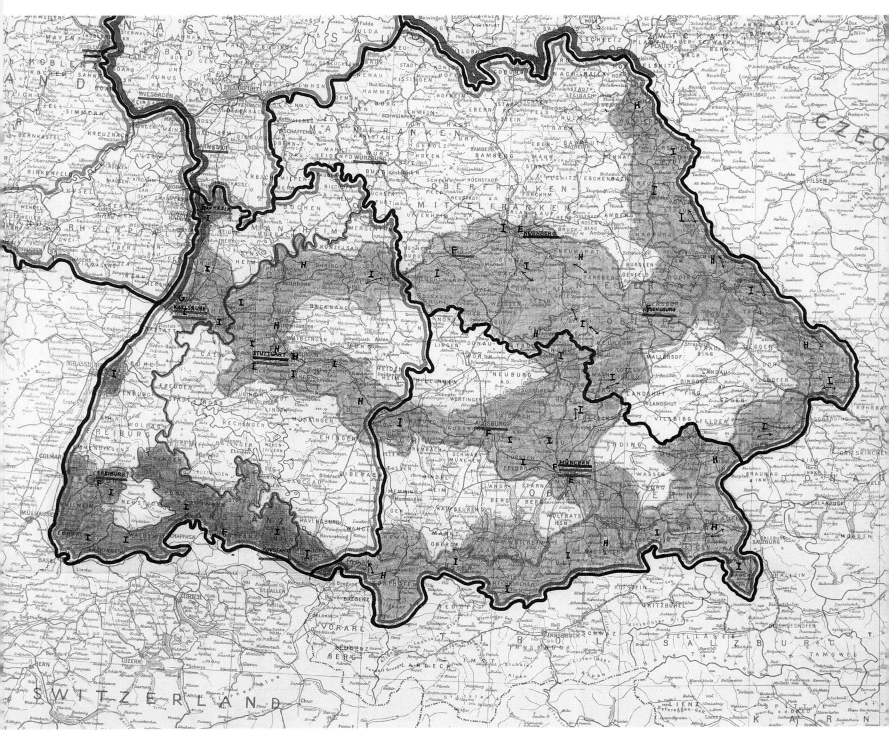

Above:

The French Military Government Map, June, 1945, was a blueprint for the Sixth Army, U.S. Zone of Occupation, and plotted the foreclosure of the Third Reich. One of a number of coded maps found in the archives of Lt. Col. Wolfson, it details a series of attacks that began in late January 1945.

Led by General Jacob L. Devers, Commander of the Sixth Army, the Allies cleared the Colmar pocket and pierced the formidable Siegfried Line west of the Rhine River. Heavy casualties were inflicted during the course of these battles. By May 6, this eastern initiative found the Sixth Army at Brenner Pass on the Swiss border. Entry into Munich and Austria was assured. Almost one million German forces surrendered to General Devers on that day.[1]

Red represented the United States; green, the combined Allied Forces. The invasion, named "Eclipse Thrust," targeted Munich and Dachau.

The alphabetical symbols are codes for the deployment of personnel. The "I" depicts detachments composed of equal amounts of officers and enlisted men occupying the perimeters of the German state. The "F" and "E" were sizeable detachments that participated in the final battles.

Sign bearing text visible in image:
- Rx TREAT... HAPPIES... RUMORS...
- FREE SPEECH doesn't mean Careless TALK!
- HAVE a HEART Leave that RUMOR On your LIPS Or On ours. Miami Beach Jaycees.
- LOOK WHO'S Listening
- Old Man RUMOR is UNFAIR to WAR EFF... Miami Beach Jaycees.
- Old Man RUMOR is UNFAIR to WAR EFFORT Miami Beach Jaycees.
- Do You Kn... MOST RUM... ARE STAR... BY O... ENEM...
- Think! THERE IS NO SUCH THING as a TRUE RUMOR Miami Beach Jaycees
- ...F YOU HAVE A GOOD RUMOR Repeat it to The F.B.I. Miami Beach Jaycees

ME
NATIO
BU

FLORIDA PO

Training Grounds

The United States government established large training centers in Miami Beach to preserve the economic structure of the community during World War II. Miami Beach was a destination for several hundred thousand soldiers in 1942 and 1943. No other training center in the country challenged Miami Beach's combination of economy and good times for the soldiers. The Beach's only industry, housing visitors, was revolutionized quickly, and the finest hotels and apartment buildings in America were leased to the Army Air Forces at the amazing low rate of $8 per person per month. The glorious climate permitted training these men and women 365 days of the year.

"Do you know that most rumors are started by our enemies"
Miami Beach Jaycees

Above:
Sign-bearing members of the Miami Beach Jaycees demonstrate against wartime rumor outside the Mercantile National Bank Building, 420 Lincoln Road, designed by Albert Anis in 1940. Gertrude and Kenneth Oka are fifth and sixth from the right. April 5, 1942.

Opposite, above:
Demonstrators wore jackets and ties in the 1940s. Kenneth Oka stands on the left side of the Rumor Board.

Opposite, below:
"Old Man Rumor" sports a silk top hat. To draw attention to their protest, the demonstrators created an effigy, "Old Man Rumor." They marched him to a curvaceous Lincoln Road palm tree, across from the Albion Hotel, and hung him in playful ceremony. The crowd consists of members of the Miami Beach Police Department, Jaycees, beauties in bathing suits, and men in uniform.

Twenty Million Pounds Melted for Munitions

When the United States entered World War II, a survey of Miami Beach was made and every possible source of scrap metal was identified. Due to the Mediterranean influence, Miami was a great source of wrought iron architectural enhancements to melt down for munitions. Residents inaugurated a drive to encourage people who had ironwork to give it up for scrap. Letters went out to owners of properties with ironworks, and trucks were sent to pick up and haul the metals to the proper authorities. The expenses were covered by a group of patriotic citizens. State of Florida officials estimated the total amount of scrap collected by The Florida Junior Army weighed twenty million pounds.[3]

Miss Florida of 1942, Eileen Knapp, helps Councilman Mitchell Wolfson dissect an iron gate for scrap metal. This attractive gate belonged to the Belle Isle estate of Mrs. Lee Rumsey, a pioneer resident who was present when Miami Beach was incorporated into a city. There were only three hundred people in Miami at that time. Mrs. Rumsey also donated her iron fence, patio railings, and iron window bars.[4]
October 25, 1942.

"I wish it were possible for every person to see an official U.S. Army film of the bombing of Shanghai. . . This film is fact and not fiction. In it you can see what could happen here. . . it is time every ostrich among us should raise his head and face actualities. This is war and was for keeps."
Mitchell Wolfson, Chairman, Special Salvage Committee for Metal Gates and Fences

The Lincoln Theatre
contributed its share to
the drive for scrap
metal for the war effort.

**"Stripped
for Defense"**
Source unknown

Stripped for Defense—

*More than a thousand pounds of satin
finish aluminum from the marquee of
the Lincoln Theatre in Miami Beach
has been turned over to Uncle Sam.
A new marquee, using baked enamel,
is being installed in the Wometco de-
luxer, managed by Sonny Shepherd.*

SPECIAL SALVAGE COMMITTEE
for
METAL GATES AND FENCES

MIAMI BEACH, FLORIDA

October 22, 1942

PLEASE ADDRESS ALL
CORRESPONDENCE TO
MITCHELL WOLFSON, CHAIRMAN
P. O. BOX 2440
MIAMI, FLORIDA

MEMBERS OF COMMITTEE

MR. F. LOWRY WALL
MR. JUDSON OWEN
MR. DAN MAHONEY
MR. JOHN MONTGOMERY
MR. BRYAN HANKS
MR. ROMEY TURRELL
MR. HUGH LARRICK
MR. WILLIAM TARADASH
MR. WALTER B. WILSON
MR. GUS GEIGER
MR. C. W. CHASE, JR.
MRS. AGNES PURNELL
MR. CHARLES CLEMENTS
MR. SAM R. BECKER
MR. LEONARD ABESS
MR. AL JOLSON
MRS. JULIO SANCHEZ
DR. MORRIS GOODMAN
MR. BEN BRONSTON
MRS. ED KEEFER
MR. CLAUDE RENSHAW
MR. VAL C. CLEARY
MR. JOHN LEVI
MR. LEE POWELL
MR. HERBERT FRINK
MR. WILLIAM BURBRIDGE
MR. ROBERT RALSTON
MR. EDGAR B. PEARCE
   VICE CHAIRMAN

Dear Citizen:

Do you want to help win the war ?   Of course you do !
And you may well feel that you are doing all that is human-
ly possible to do your share - even more than your share.

The writer of this letter feels as you do about it, but
these are serious times - no one's work or sacrifice is
over - ours at home or the boys over there, until the
peace is won.

But here is the story - In cooperation with the Dade County Salvage Committee, a group of prominent Miami Beach
citizens, Presidents of Civic Clubs, Banks, Chamber of
Commerce and City Officials, are making every effort to
have the City of Miami Beach do its share in the drive
for scrap metal.

You have ornamental metal on your property (a gate, a fence
or both).   Will you toss these in the heap ? We realize
that this is a costly sacrifice and a true test of patriot-
ism, but this war needs just such unselfishness.   Will
you join your committee and most every other Miami Beach
property owner who is scrapping ornamental metal gates or
fences for munitions ?

Remember, if the Jap or Hitler come, GATES CANNOT KEEP HIM
OUT OF YOUR HOME - but as guns, tanks and shells, THEY WILL
KEEP HIM OUT OF YOUR COUNTRY !

You can say "Yes" on this same sheet of paper and send it
back to us.   We will take down the iron and haul it away.
Just advise if you want to contribute your iron gate, your
fence, or both.

Cordially yours,

Mitchell Wolfson, Chairman

mw/at

129

Minus A Thousand Pounds

The Lincoln Theatre, 555 Lincoln Road, was designed in 1935 by Robert E. Collins and T.W. Lamb. In its first five years, the Lincoln staged more premiers than any theatre in the country outside of Hollywood. More than a thousand pounds of satin finish aluminum was stripped from the marquee of the Lincoln Theatre on Lincoln Road and donated to Uncle Sam by Womecto for the war effort. A new marquee of baked enamel, pictured on the right, was installed as a replacement.

Wometco to the Front

Months after the successful completion of the scrap metal drive, volunteers were called from South Florida to "make sure that enemy bombers will never be able to sneak over South Florida as they sneaked over Pearl Harbor." The call came from the Miami Army Information center, a clearing house for reports from airplane observation posts throughout strategic South Florida. Six hundred people were needed to run the center, working three hour shifts around the clock. First to sign up were fourteen men from Wometco, including Mitchell Wolfson. The information center had a complete Wometco shift.[5]

Wometco came to the front in other ways as well. Its facilities were made available for visual education programs necessary to Officer Candidate Training. At the conclusion of daily classes, the servicemen were admitted to Wometco movie houses for less than half price and were allowed to take dates or wives at the same low price. Each theater also became a War Bond issuing agent and gained an unsurpassed record for the sale of bonds.

Wometco Theatres
P. O. BOX 2440
PHONE 2-6262
306 NORTH MIAMI AVENUE
MIAMI 31, FLORIDA

"I would not leave my family, my business, you all, the Mayor's job, etc., etc., for a million dollars to ten million in cash. There is nothing in the world that I want or would induce me to leave except one, and only one thing . . . As a Jew, I thank God daily and each night that our family and our children can enjoy the blessings of this great country. After all, why are we born and allowed to live? The belief is so that we can make it a little better for those who come after us. Certainly not for pleasure and good times alone.

"My heart really prompts me to serve this, my country, if she needs me. I don't believe I could ever be happy, satisfied, or not ashamed of myself, if I turned down an opportunity to serve. Just what I can or will do to destroy Hitler and his terrible ideas, I don't know, but I should not turn down the opportunity. If I do, I believe I will live to regret it. Even in the last war, we did not have the Jewish question. In this war, we have that, and also the duty to our county."[6]

Rationing Style

The war penetrated every aspect of daily life. Mrs. Wolfson was also swept up in patriotic zeal. With much of the nation, she enthusiastically supported programs limiting use of products at home in order to help the Boys abroad. Regulation L-85, passed in 1943, affected all clothing made out of materials deemed important for the war effort. Much of WWII was fought in the air. Silk was a vital material, used for parachutes and survival maps carried by air force pilots. Women gave up silk underwear. Shoes could only be purchased with a ration ticket.

The application of Regulation L-85 to women's clothing limited the amount of fabric to be used. L-85 determined the length of suit jackets, the width of pants, and the narrowing of skirts. The hem depth of skirts was not allowed to exceed two inches, and the width of belts was limited as well. Dress designers met the challenge by creating wartime staples of narrow dress, broad shoulders, and skirts made interesting with a pleat or two. They found themselves using even less material than allowed. The lean silhouette gave them the opportunity to develop what they laughingly referred to as "austerity fashions."

Left:
The Roney Plaza hotel was the site of the Farewell Party on September 22, 1943. Seven hundred citizens said goodbye to newly commissioned Major Wolfson. Wolfson departed for training at Camp Custer, Michigan, before shipping off to Europe. The party was arranged by civic leaders, and many young women who worked for Wometco volunteered to serve at the punch bowls.

Hollywood provided a new model of glamour, and the movies of the period fixed in the mind a new silhouette by the world renowned Adrian: broad shouldered top, pencil-thin skirt, and a new sense of height. Hair was rolled inches above the forehead to accommodate the high crowned hats that topped this vertical presentation. The outfits were typically worn with daintier accessories like graduated strings of pearls and silk lapel flowers. For Frances Wolfson, Florida supplied the originals and left the silk to the war effort. Since cotton also had its military uses, pliable synthetic jerseys made with various draped effects were popular. Opting for sparer fashions not only freed materials but left pocket money for buying war savings bonds.

Eclipse Thrust
A pencil sketch, 1945, on tracing paper found in the packet of information provided to the Allied leaders for the final campaign, "Eclipse Thrust." The map details Eastern Germany and part of western Austria. It was carried by Lt. Col. Wolfson and brought home when he returned a year later.

Opposite:
Mitchell Wolfson
in field uniform

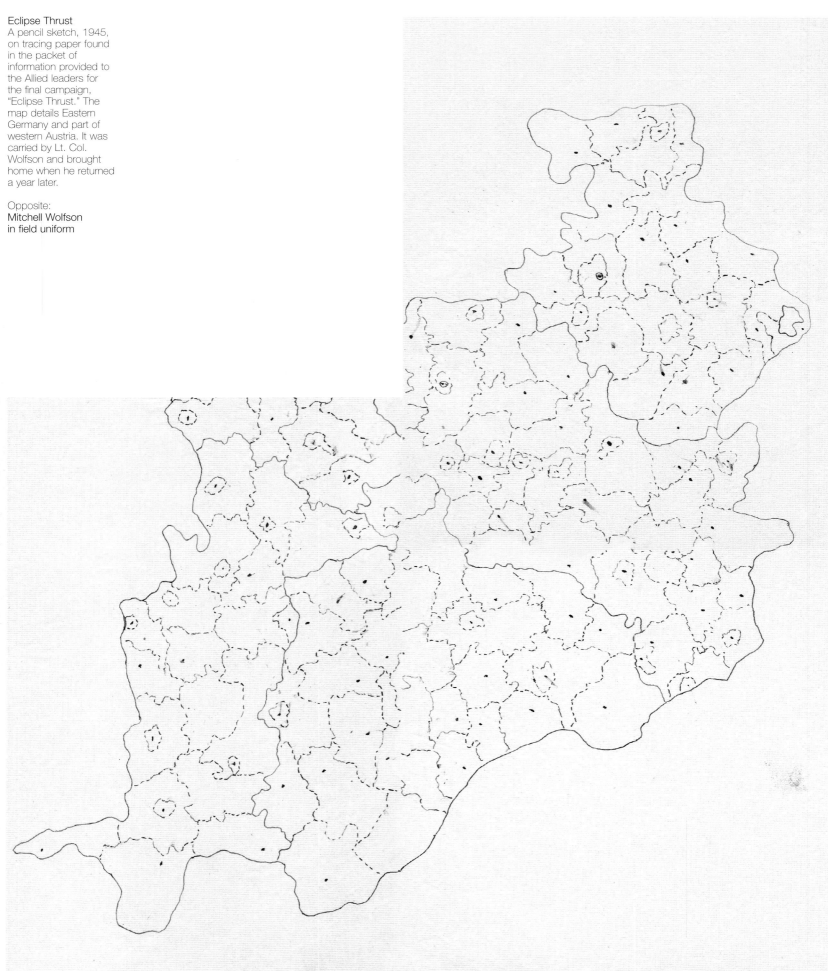

Action and Observation

Within sixty days from the time that Mitchell Wolfson enlisted, he was sent overseas—first to England and then to North Africa, where he served with the Seventh Army. Wolfson participated in the invasion of Southern France and its subsequent liberation as commander of operations from Marseilles to Lyon. Continuing all the way up through Germany to Heidelberg, he found himself at various points in these campaigns with the Third Division, the Thirty-sixth Division, and the Forty-fifth Division. He marched into Munich with the Seventh Army and entered Braun House, Hitler's home. Mitchell Wolfson participated in the decision to destroy the house so that it couldn't become a museum or shrine. Several things were removed from Braun House before the Army blew it up, including Hitler's sterling silver personal knife, fork, and spoon. These were presented to Wolfson and brought back to 5030 North Bay Road in Miami Beach.

After the fall of Munich, Lt. Col. Wolfson entered Dachau with a corps of soldiers hardened by battle and toughened by life in the trenches. But nothing prepared them for the sight of the death camp. In an extensive oral memoir, Wolfson described how these soldiers cried like babies. The odor of dead bodies was unbelievable, although experienced, hard to imagine, and impossible to process.

After Germany surrendered to the Allies, Wolfson's Sixth Army Group went into every single town of over five thousand people to investigate whether or not Nazis were still in political control. The first stop was always the police station. Then City Hall. The occupying forces were interested in the solvency of the banks. A questionnaire, called a Fragebogen, was filled out by all citizens. Thirty years later, Wolfson recalled that no one ever admitted to being a Nazi. Mitchell Wolfson surveyed the destruction and chaos around him; displaced persons, food supplies interrupted, town after town completely ruined. Wolfson respected the enemy, and observed that by systematically destroying the lines of communication, the Allies had defeated a German army consisting of fine and brave soldiers. As part of the reconstruction team, Wolfson was assigned the task of rebuilding the networks of transmittal and conveyance.

This gave him further opportunity to process his thoughts regarding all that he had been part of, all he had observed during the past two years of war. Wolfson concluded that communications were perhaps the most important element in any civilization. And, certainly, in his future. He considered how and to what benefit he could utilize this perception to help Wometco enter the business of communication.

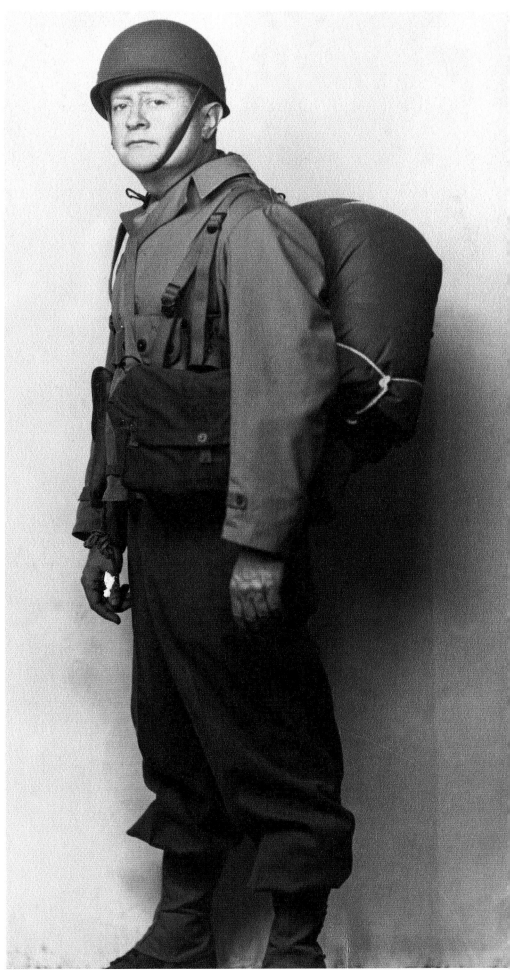

Lt. Col. Mitchell Wolfson receiving the **Bronze Star**, May 25, 1945.

War Hero

Lt. Col. Mitchell Wolfson received the Bronze Star medal for "meritorious achievement" for his participation in the army from September 15, 1944 to May 12, 1945 in France and Germany. He was decorated by General Jacob L. Devers, Commander of the Sixth Army in Heidelberg, Germany. The citation that accompanied the medal noted his outstanding services in planning and supervising both civil affairs and military government. The Colonel's tireless energy, a quality he carried with him all of his life, was also praised. At the same time, the Colonel was awarded the French government's Croix de Guerre for services performed for the French Army.

Lt. Col. Wolfson receiving the **Croix de Guerre**, May 25, 1945.

Left:
Sent by Major Wolfson to the family he left back in Miami Beach, December 1944.

« If Russia puts th[e] men on the moon, w[e] counter with a wom[an]

A Cold War Gag
This cartoon, scribbled on the notepad on Kenneth Oka's desk, was not discarded as scrap, but carefully filed away. It captures the zeitgeist of the Sputnik Era. Unknown cartoonist c. 1958

THE WOLFSONIAN FOUNDATION

1001 Washington Avenue
Miami Beach, Florida 33139
(305) 531-1001
Telex: 9102504230
U.S.A.

Castello Mackenzie-Wolfson
Casella Postale: 1367
16122 Genova
Uffici:
Via Roccatagliata Ceccardi, 1
16121 Genova
(010) 564916 – 17–18
Italia

Michele,

Cut outs? Who are these icons of
fashion? Are these people we know or are
they dolls? I don't think I'm the type
to fit the costume to the figure. Do you
mind sending me a fashion plate with the
dressmaker's models so I can watch the
sartorial parade? I wish I was more
conscious about clothes but somehow I
only got as far as the 346 shop on the
third floor of Brooks Brothers New York
store. After that I was left to my own
fashion devices and I put on what I came
to here and there during my travels.
It's only fair that you enlighten me
about style on the Beach.

Micky

Previous spread:
Travelling in Style
Mitchell Wolfson and his son Louis return from Nassau, June 17, 1940. Note the elephant hide briefcase. The dark, distinct texture contrasts with the delicate weave of the natural straw Panama hat. Young Louis is correctly attired in his double breasted blazer and hat.

Page 140/141:
More Hollywood than Miami Beach
Most probably a theme evening sponsored by the Jaycees, possibly at the Bali Club. The faux palms, volcanic mountains, anthurium leaves, and dark goddesses arrived from the South Seas via the silver screen to inspire this tropical evening. The gardenias were probably local. A young Kenneth Oka is third from right, standing.

First Lady
A portrait shot for the public record, the First Lady of Miami Beach in June 1943. Surrounded by flowers and adorned with pearls, Frances Wolfson is radiant in a silk print of stylized vegetation. The dress was the natural look more typical of the 1930s than the 40s, with waistline placed at the natural waist and given little emphasis. Her brown hair is in a classic style of the 1940s, gently rolled above the forehead. This official portrait appeared in all of the local newspapers.

Fashionable First Ladies

Opposite:
"The Fish and I"
Gertrude's notation in the family scrapbook. She revealed that she didn't actually catch the fish. She spotted the photo op while visiting Everglades National Park, and posed with bandanna, white cotton peasant blouse and the silvery tarpon. A great sport fish, the silver king *(Tarpon atlanticus)*, dashes and leaps in the water; its large scales glisten in the sunlight like molten silver. Tarpon is not considered a good fish to eat, as its flesh is dry and coarse.

Below:
Seminole Goddess
State of Florida Seal, 1953. The Seminole goddess is the eternal First Lady of Florida.

Inside left page, from left to right:

Gertrude Oka in a pale blue chiffon dress with applique leaves, 1945.

Gertrude Oka in a cotton pique hibiscus print, 1941. The vine in the background *(Thunbergia grandiflora)* provides a sweep of foliage and is often used in Florida to cover and climb.

At the engagement party for her oldest son, Louis II, Frances Wolfson wears a fashionable ballerina-length dress with a black lace mantilla draped over the shoulders and clasped with a triple orchid corsage, 1951.

Gertrude Oka with a popular poodle cut hair-do and a floral silk print dress at the Deauville Hotel, c. 1950s.

Frances Wolfson lifts her glass to holiday cheer in a white two-piece outfit with red strawberries. A narrow belt matches a narrow band at the collar.

Frances Wolfson at the Symphony Club's Flamingo Ball, Hialeah Race Track, March 1, 1957. **"Looking like the modern muse of music . . . an inspiration in her white silk damask ball gown with hand-painted morning glories scattered over the full skirt, and blue chiffon defining the bodice and forming a stole, President of the Symphony Club, beguiling Frances was thrilled with the turn out . . .**

While presiding in this dress, Frances told the audience: 'Our community has left the frontier stage of its development. Better educational and cultural facilities for the development of mind and spirit are equally important with drives to improve the health standards of a community.'" Unidentified newspaper article

Inside right page, from left to right:

Gertrude Oka in a black silk sheath with thin belt aboard the Costa Cruise Line's Franca C at Port Everglades for a week's cruise to Jamaica and Haiti in 1961. The sheath silhouette evolved into the prevailing style of the 1960s, exemplified by Audrey Hepburn as Holly Golightly in "Breakfast at Tiffany's."

A formal **Mrs. Wolfson** in an off-the-shoulder ball gown at a Soirée Symphonique.

A formal **Mrs. Oka** at the Coronation Ball of the Miss Universe Pageant, July 14, 1962, at the Fontainebleau. Mrs. Oka's dress, by Soli Moustaki in pink and gold silk, was created from an Indian sari Gertrude had purchased while traveling.
"In Paris you make a dress in 40 hours. In Miami, you learn to make a dress in 40 minutes." Soli Moustak

The hostess, Frances Wolfson, in a hand-kerchief style strapless evening dress, checking her reflection in a beautiful filigree compact before her guests arrive, 1949.

Gertrude Oka attending a fashion showing of Esteban Mayo, a designer from Mexico City. His collection showed the influence of traditional Aztec designs and craftsmanship, translated into modern styles. One thousand women viewed the showing.

Perpetual
Fan System

The ocean breezes
move continuously
across the peninsula
of Florida from the east,
southeast, and south.
They function as a
perpetual fan system,
distributing a constant
supply of fresh air.
Generated by the
movement of the earth's
rotation, these Trade
Winds call up a
dimension of excitement
and expectation—
a sense of being
airborne. Leaves drift by,
trees move, and birds
play with the currents.

Opposite:
Ocean Breezes

Gertrude flying her
colors in the tropical
Trade Winds, 1940,
La Gorce Circle.
Gertrude holds a
nautical style scarf to
the skies. The diamond
pattern of the scarf
and the checkerboard
of her shorts combine
in a playful geometry.
This is the era of the
sweater girl, when
Hollywood's favorite
pin-ups were Lana
Turner and Rita
Hayworth.

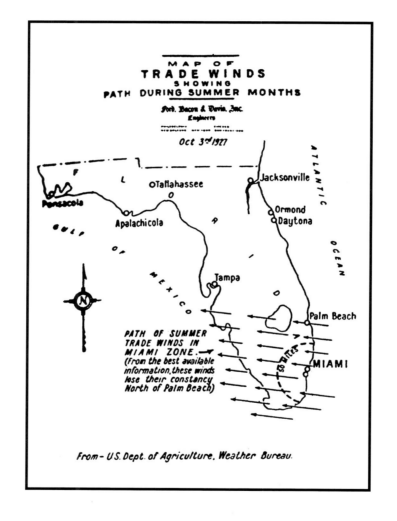

Major Stoles

Gathering of glamour at the Carib Theater, probably a University of Miami Symphony Club event. Fur stoles became fashionable in the 1930s, when women favored long gowns and coat lengths looked too short. In the daytime, mink was the fur of choice, and in the evening an ermine or sable was preferred. Stoles went out of fashion in the 1960s, as hemlines came way up.

From left to right, with white gloves:

Ranch mink (natural mink) long straight stole

Mink capelet, possibly cerulean or diadem, worn by Florence Pick, President of the Symphony Club when it was founded in the early 1950s

White ermine bolero with a shawl collar

Nancy Green in a white mink jacket with a big cape collar

Mink stole, autumn haze, 60-inch length, long straight stole

Zenia Meyers in a sable stole

Frances Wolfson sans fur

Ranch mink capelet worn by Marie Volpe, grande dame, U.M. Symphony Orchestra, and author of *Music in Miami*, an autobiography

Janet Atlas in ermine bolero with small shawl collar

White fox stole

Sunglasses

As far back as the 1930s, sunglasses were marketed as part of the mid-winter uniform for tourists who were coming to Miami Beach. In the late 1930s, Chanel donned oversized sunglasses in gray Paris and when Garbo, too, appeared with them in public, sunglasses as fashion were launched. In the 1950s, they became an art form. Cellulose acetate, the most commonly used plastic for eyeglass frames, could be injection molded. Mass production began. Fashion accessories proliferated after the sparse sensibility of World War II, when any excess was considered unpatriotic. In addition to sunglasses, gloves, hats, handbags, stoles, and shoes were part of "The Outfit."

Madame Chiang Kai-shek, the youngest and most famous of the three glamorous Soong sisters ("one loved money, one loved power, one loved China," a ditty went), visited Miami to meet with George Storer of Storer broadcasting. Storer was known to be a great supporter of her husband, General Chiang Kai-shek. In February 1943, Madame Chiang Kai-shek addressed both houses of Congress in Washington, D.C. The second woman ever accorded that honor, she reportedly wore sheer hose, high heels, and red-tipped fingers. As a guest of the Roosevelts at the White House, she brought her own silk sheets and had them changed daily. She shocked Eleanor Roosevelt at a White House dinner when asked how the Chinese government would handle a strike by coal miners. Madame Chiang drew a sharp red fingernail across her neck. "She can talk beautifully about democracy," Mrs. Roosevelt said later, "but she does not know how to live democracy." Madame Chiang outlived every one of her enemies. She spent her final years in New York City in an apartment at Gracie Square, occupied with the study of watercolor paintings. She lived 105 years and died in 2003.[1]

Opposite:
Madame Chiang Kai-shek, with her characteristic red nails. Gertrude Oka, left, wears a grey shantung silk suit from Bergdorf Goodman in New York. In the 1960s, silk shantung was often used as a daytime fabric. Suit jackets were tailored, and so defined at the waist that they almost form peplums. They had fairly short, "bracelet-length" sleeves, in order to accommodate long gloves which gathered at the wrists. Skirts were narrow. Madame Chiang Kai-shek, right, carries a European style crocodile bag with her traditional Chinese dress.

Barbara June Oka in a **Little Bo Peep** outfit by Sylvia Whyte.

Opposite:
Five
Crowned by a wreath of small white flowers and sporting a multi-rose corsage, five-year-old Stephanie Oka blows out the candles on a five-tiered cake marking the fifth birthday of the State of Israel—April 20, 1953. Israel's birthday was celebrated in Miami Beach with a fund-raising gala for Israel Bonds held at the Empress Hotel.

The Daughters Wore Sylvia Whyte

At the close of World War II, Sylvia Whyte opened an exclusive retail shop on Lincoln Road that was an instant success. Trained as an art student at Cooper Union in New York, Sylvia decided to enter the field of design instead of the fine arts. It was difficult to get work in those days, but a dress that she designed for her own daughter began Whyte's career. During the postwar 1940s and early 1950s, celebrities flocked to Sylvia Whyte's shop. Debbie Reynolds bought dresses for her daughter, Carrie Fisher. Nat King Cole shopped for his daughter, Natalie. Zsa Zsa Gabor purchased clothes for Francesca, her child with Conrad Hilton. Frank Sinatra bought suits for Frank Jr. and dresses for Nancy Jr. and Tina.

Politicians's wives shopped as well. The wife of Cuba's infamous dictator Fulgencio Batista made frequent trips to clothe their children, and Mrs. Perez Jiminez of Venezuela traveled to Lincoln Road as well. In later years, Whyte designed for the Kennedys, Johnsons, Carters, and George Bush's grandchildren. "Better stores" all over the country still carry Sylvia Whyte designs. In 1988, Saks Fifth Avenue celebrated twenty-five years of glorious friendship with Sylvia Whyte. In 1993 Whyte was named one of the twenty-five most influential women in children's clothing.

Overtures to Culture

"Today I am
convinced that
music, in any
shape or form, is
one of the greatest
things man has
developed for his
own entertainment
and uplifting.
I like all kinds of
music, from the
samba or rumba
to the symphony,
and my favorite
is the string
quartet. I think
that to study music
is very important
for children,
not only for the
training they get,
but because it
teaches them to
live with other
children."
Kenneth Oka[1]

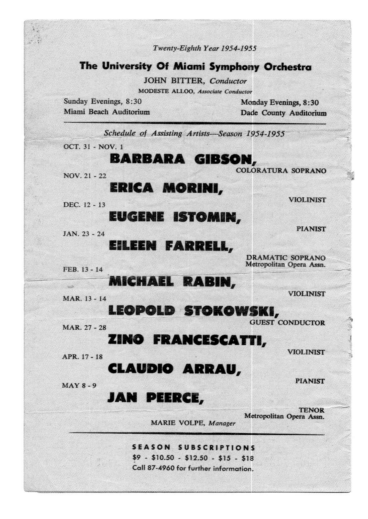

Twenty-Eighth Year 1954-1955

The University Of Miami Symphony Orchestra

JOHN BITTER, *Conductor*

MODESTE ALLOO, *Associate Conductor*

Sunday Evenings, 8:30   Monday Evenings, 8:30
Miami Beach Auditorium   Dade County Auditorium

Schedule of Assisting Artists—Season 1954-1955

OCT. 31 - NOV. 1

BARBARA GIBSON,
COLORATURA SOPRANO

NOV. 21 - 22

ERICA MORINI,
VIOLINIST

DEC. 12 - 13

EUGENE ISTOMIN,
PIANIST

JAN. 23 - 24

EILEEN FARRELL,
DRAMATIC SOPRANO
Metropolitan Opera Assn.

FEB. 13 - 14

MICHAEL RABIN,
VIOLINIST

MAR. 13 - 14

LEOPOLD STOKOWSKI,
GUEST CONDUCTOR

MAR. 27 - 28

ZINO FRANCESCATTI,
VIOLINIST

APR. 17 - 18

CLAUDIO ARRAU,
PIANIST

MAY 8 - 9

JAN PEERCE,
TENOR
Metropolitan Opera Assn.

MARIE VOLPE, *Manager*

SEASON SUBSCRIPTIONS
$9 - $10.50 - $12.50 - $15 - $18
Call 87-4960 for further information.

Michele,

I've discovered that Miami Beach is the object of some of the worst poetic drivel ever composed. And imagine, the authors are some of the most prominent and accomplished poets and writers of their day.

For example, in 1916, the poet Laureate of Indiana, James Whitcomb Riley, was invited by Carl Fisher, formerly of Indianapolis, to commemorate the civilizing of the mangrove swamp and the incorporation of Miami Beach into a city. Riley, whose works had earned him the title "poet of the common people," composed a poem for the occasion. A ceremonial planting of a young ficus tree took place on Lincoln Road. Riley presented the following words to the new community:

We plant this tree
Beside the sea
In trust, that it yet may wave
Through shower and shade
In sunny hours
For other eyes as glad as ours.

Riley enjoyed his visit to Miami Beach and spent the last three winters of his life in Miami. Sadly the tree no longer exists.

On the other hand, Michele, culture on the Beach was like an underground movement that surfaced when called upon, good spirited and ever present but nascent. Until recently it was never a primary activity though the settlers had talent like your father who played the violin and my mother who had quite a good voice. In fact like a siren of yore, she captured Mitchell through her singing. Lots of them knew even if what they knew went unpracticed. What's important here, Michele, is the picture of a community with cultural resources sufficient to stimulate and to prepare our intellectual faculties. In other words, we were part of a cultural overture which set the stage for development.

Micky

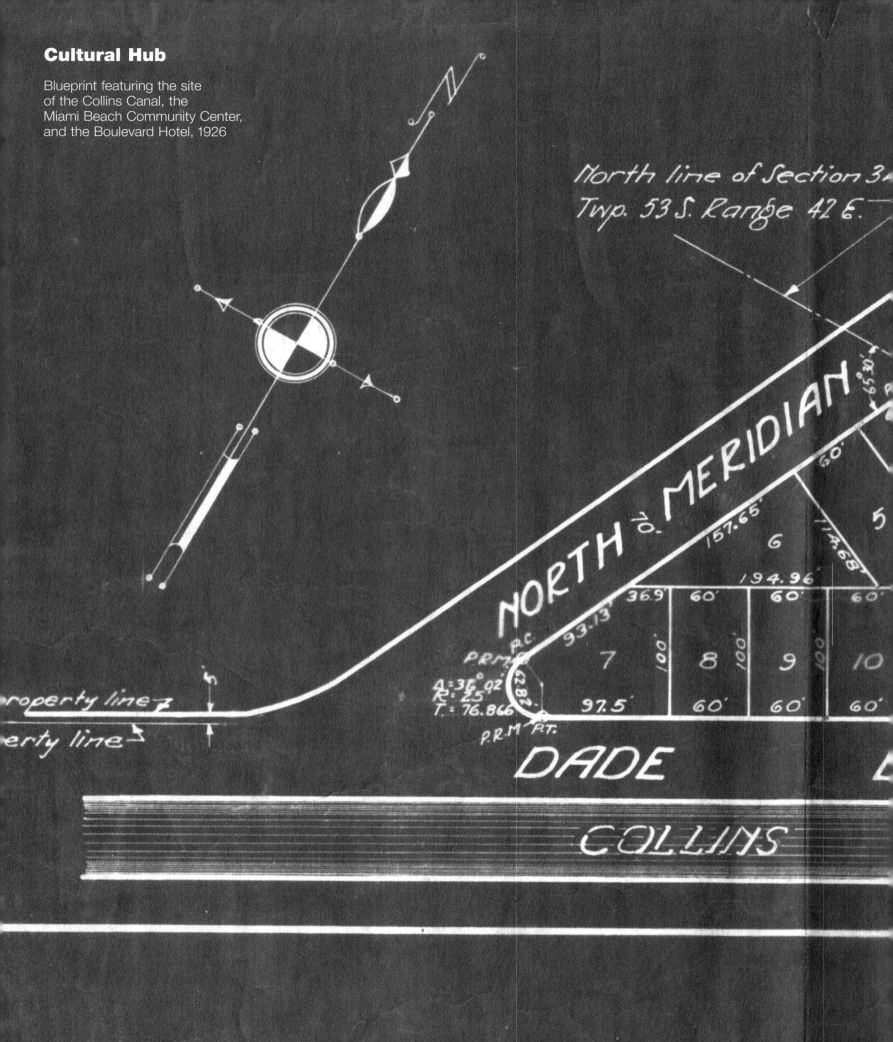

Cultural Hub

Blueprint featuring the site
of the Collins Canal, the
Miami Beach Community Center,
and the Boulevard Hotel, 1926

North line of Lot 1 Blk. 1 Mid-Golf
Subdivision as Recorded in Plat book 4
at Page 200 of Public Records Dade
County Florida

A Canal and Venetian Gondolas

The Miami Beach Community Center was designed by architect August Geiger in 1916. At 2100 Washington Avenue, it occupied a prime piece of real estate adjacent to Collins Canal, the main aquatic thoroughfare. The Canal, begun in 1912, links Biscayne Bay with Lake Pancoast. John Collins, early developer and visionary, dreamed of transporting fruits from the tropical tree orchards he envisioned springing up in Miami Beach. This dream was never realized. However, a year later Collins built the longest wooden bridge in the world, connecting 15th Street in Miami to Dade Boulevard.

The connecting bridge inspired a new era of romantic fantasy for Carl Fisher. The canal was now used to transport clients interested in Miami Beach real estate and recreation. Fisher imported black gondolas from Venice, hired photographers, and notified the world at large that Miami Beach was a dream awaiting the adventuresome and curious. The orchards became Orchard Subdivision, and houses sprang up.

The Community Center was originally Carl Fisher's Miami Beach Municipal Golf Course House. In the 1950s, it was used by the community for classes in visual and performing arts. At one point, the center was active enough to maintain its own teaching staff. Local children spent after-school hours and Saturday mornings studying ceramics, dance, or drama.

The rear entrance to the **Miami Beach Community Center,** at the south side of the Collins Canal. The steps to the boat dock no longer exist. The front entrance, now obscured by municipal development, previously faced an expanse of golf greens. However, during the 1950s, their greens were used as a play field for the children attending the center. Shige Tashiro's Miami Beach Nurseries was one of the primary landscapers.

Below:
Ceramic rendition of a beach ball, signed Barbara June Oka, c. 1955. The three Oka girls made dozens of ceramic objects during the mid 1950s, including a number of life-size hibiscus, with stamen tipped with soft clay pressed through a fine sieve to resemble pollen-generating anther and filaments.

Modern and Creative Dance

Modern dance typified the innovative spirit of the times
and individual expression of American life in the post-war
years. Judith Youngerman studied with Anita Zahn, a
protégée of Isadora Duncan, and also trained with Martha
Graham, Jose Limon, and Jay Dudley. Miss Youngerman
brought to Miami Beach a new and exciting art form.
For several years Judith Youngerman taught classes in
Modern and Creative dance to adults and children in
Miami Beach. She was associated with the Miami Beach
Community Center staff and later held classes across
the Collins Canal at the Boulevard Hotel.

**Lengthening
and Strengthening
the Body**
Modern dance teacher
Judith Youngerman with
students demonstrating
leg extensions at the
Boulevard Hotel, 1952.
Barbara June Oka
is in second row right;
Michele Lee Oka,
first row right.

166

Miami's Musical Matriarch

Mana-Zucca was Miami's musical matriarch. At the age of eight, she created a sensation in New York by playing a Beethoven piano concerto with the New York Symphony Orchestra under the direction of Walter Damrosch. Composing came naturally as well; Mana-Zucca wrote her first concerto at the age of seventeen. She wrote a thousand works—serious concertos, sonatas, and popular songs including "I Love Life," a song that made her briefly famous. Jascha Heifetz and Misha Elman have performed her works for the violin.

Red poinsettias and pink oleanders predominated at Mana-Zucca's wedding to Irwin Cassel, a prominent Miami retailer. For the occasion, she penned a fitting composition entitled "If Flowers Could Speak." Throughout the years, Mana-Zucca devoted time, energy, and money to developing and promoting music in Miami. Even the nearby Everglades appealed to her creative sensibilities. Mana-Zucca evoked the Great Spirit to realize "Seminole Lullaby," an enchanting melody that incorporated Native American words and myths. She was an organizer of the University of Miami Symphony in 1926. Her friend Arnold Volpe from New York was to be the conductor.

Her Miami house, Mazica Hall, at the site of the present-day Omni International Hotel, was a showplace where audiences filled her eighty-foot living room to hear live music. Fritz Kreisler, Alma Gluck, and Ephrem Zimbalist, considered the cream of the musical crop, sometimes performed at her Tuesday concerts. The cellist Leonard Rose made his debut in her home.

Mana-Zucca collected pianos. Two were concert grands, but the rest were miniatures that she found all over the world. They ranged from a reproduction of Mozart's harpsichord and beautifully detailed Dresden, Meissen, silver and ivory pieces, to a folk art piano carved out of an old cigar box. She owned the first piano brought to this country by John Jacob Astor, a miniature scribbled on by Oscar Strauss, a descendant of the famous waltzing Strausses. Included in this collection is the piano that started it all—a plywood model carved by her son when he was a child.

Mana-Zucca and her piano collection.

Opposite:
Sheet music cover for **"Seminole Lullaby,"** 1941. The beautiful lithographic cover depicts a swampy Everglades at bedtime.

Following spreads: Sheet music for **"Seminole Lullaby" and "My Florida,"** composed by Mana-Zucca. The words for "My Florida" were written in 1937 by Vivian Yeiser Laramore, appointed Florida Poet Laureate for life in 1931. She edited "Miami Muse," a poetry column in the Miami *Daily News*, and compiled a number of anthologies that became the creative voice of Florida poets.

Laramore left a legacy of poems celebrating the sensuous nature of South Florida, including *Poinciana Poems*, published by Pandanus Press in 1953. Her work was celebrated for its passion and wizardry with words.

MANA-ZUCCA

SEMINOLE LULLABY

Poem By Emma Roberts Wilson

<u>HIGH</u> 40¢ LOW

ELKAN-VOGEL CO. ·· PUBLISHERS ··· PHILA., PA

To Elsa Baklor

SEMINOLE LULLABY

Poem by
Emma Roberts Wilson

Music by
Mana-Zucca, Op. 145

Sleep lit-tle wood pid-geon, while in the west, The young hunt-er's moon goes slow-ly to rest; Est-to-chee,* Est-to-chee, slum-ber and sleep, Est-to-chee, slum-ber and sleep.

Now in your bear skin, warm-ly I fold you, Deep in my heart, safe-ly I hold you;

* "Est-to-chee" is a Seminole word meaning "Baby"
(ch – pronounced as in cheek) Copyright 1941 by Elkan-Vogel Co., Inc. Philadelphia, Pa.
International Copyright Secured

High V.

MY FLORIDA

Lyric by
VIVIAN YEISER LARAMORE

Music by
MANA–ZUCCA Op. 155

un-du-la-ting Ev-er-glades, Your mer-ry mock-ers ser-a-nades; Your

red hi-bis-cus and the reach Of laugh-ing waves a - long the beach, A

par-a-dise where pe-tals part____ You are A-mer-i-ca's sweet-heart; My

Flor-i-da! My Flor - i - da! ____ O -da!

IN THE FLORIDA SUNSHINE

Music by

MANA=ZUCCA

Words by

DAVE OPPENHEIM

and

HENRY TOBIAS

COMPLIMENTARY

PAULL-PIONEER
Music Corporation
1657 BROADWAY, NEW YORK

Winners

"In the Florida Sunshine" was written for and dedicated to Senator Spessard Holland, a State senator campaigning for Governor. The song premiered at a rally in Flamingo Park, Miami Beach, on April 13, 1940 with Mitchell Wolfson presiding over the festivities. Spessard Holland won the election and became the 28th Governor of the Florida, serving from January 7, 1941 through January 2, 1945. The song was a winner as well, remembered long after the election had ended.

Mana-**Z**ucca **I**rwin **Ca**ssel

175

Violin Virtuoso Called Miami Home

Violin Virtuoso Joan Field, who called Miami home, was a blood relative as well as spiritual descendant of John Field (1782 to 1837), the renowned Irish pianist, teacher and composer. John wrote the first piano pieces called "nocturnes," evoking night moods. The form of these works were appropriated by his contemporary, Chopin. While John's nocturnes were said to feel the same by night and by day, Chopin's were characterized by moods that deepened as the shades of night fell. Most of John's compositions were considered to be in advance of their time, and as a result were less accessible to his contemporaries. He enjoyed greater fame as a teacher and performer. One of his celebrated students was Rachmaninoff's grandfather Vassili, who, in turn, was a great creative force in the younger Rachmaninoff's life. And in the era of great English poetry, John Field discovered the poetic capabilities of the pianoforte.

Joan was also related to the late-nineteenth century American poet Eugene Field, a Victorian best known for his children's poems. "Pittypat and Tippytoe," a lyrical verse which appeared in *Poems of Childhood*, Charles Scribner and Sons, 1904, was illustrated by Maxfield Parrish. "Wynken, Blynken, and Nod" has become an American classic. When Eugene Field died at the turn of the century, a newspaper account speculated that, "all the children of the land mourn their laureate."[2]

Joan studied with Jacques Thibaud, Albert Spalding, and Michel Piastro. She made her symphonic debut with the New York Philharmonic under Sir John Barbirolli at the age of sixteen. Her recital debut was at New York's Town Hall, where she became a frequent performer. In 1943 Joan Field was the Concert Mistress of the Ballet Russe de Monte Carlo. At her triumphant Carnegie Hall concert in 1945, she displayed her ability to create programs of unusual interest. Joan performed Giuseppe Tartini, Ludwig Spohr, Nicolai Berezowsky, Charles Sydney Freed, her mentor Albert Spalding, and concluded the concert with "Jamaican Rhumba" by Arthur Benjamin.

From the inception of her career, Joan Field championed contemporary music and has to her credit several important "First Performances." This includes the Charles Ives Violin Sonata No. 1, for which she played the first live radio broadcast performance as well as the first concert performance. Field also owned the original manuscript copy autographed to her by Mr. Ives (1874 to 1954), and played it in memoriam the year of his death. Another world premier was the Violin Concerto in D Major, op. 224 by Miami's Mana-Zucca, with the American Symphony of New York at the Brooklyn Museum Sculpture Court. Reviewed the next day, the writer complimented Miss Field for her fluent interpretation of the Mana-Zucca work, "singing out its old fashioned melodies with utmost sweetness and snapping briskly through the passages of staccato." She proceeded to appear with the Detroit, St. Louis, and Washington, D.C. symphony orchestras, and Field played for President and Mrs. Roosevelt at the White House.

Her instrument of choice was a Stradivarius, c. 1698, valued at $35,000 in the 1950s. This extraordinary violin accompanied her around the world. She played recitals and radio concerts in The Hague, Frankfurt, Cologne, and Vienna. In Sweden she performed the Sibelius Violin Concerto, winning the audience with the nobility of her interpretation. She recorded for the European Telefunken-Decca label. One of her most popular discs featured the Bruch Concerto for Violin and Orchestra No. 1 in G Minor, op. 26 and the Spohr Concerto for Violin and Orchestra No. 8 in A Minor, op. 47, performed with Rudolf Albert and the Berlin Symphony. This disc was obtainable in both hi fi and the new stereophonic sound.

In addition to projecting herself on the international stages of the world, Joan Field was keenly interested in aiding young musicians. She "concertized" to help support scholarship funds.

Shouldering Her Stradivarius
Program cover for a performance at Carnegie Hall. The playbill from the performance quoted New York *Herald-Tribune* music critic Virgil Thomson, who said of Miss Field:
"Firm in tone and rhythm, intelligent, elegant, solidly impressive. One would like to hear more violin playing of this sort."

Eulogizing his mother on March 17, 1988, David Reskin said,
"Great musicians are really after all like little children; all that matters is playing. . . She was the best kind of teacher: one who instructs by example. . . She was an old world musician, no fancy conservatory education, no gadgets. Just blind talent, ambition and years of hard work. . . She knew what was most important about being alive . . ."

CARNEGIE HALL

JOAN FIELD

186-3-6E-45   ALFRED SCOTT · PUBLISHER · 156 FIFTH AVENUE, NEW YORK

High Notes of Pleasure

The Miami Beach Auditorium, at 1700 Washington, right above Lincoln Road, was built in 1948 by architects L. Murray Dixon, Henry Hohouser, and Russell T. Pancoast. Before the construction of an auditorium, residents journeyed to Miami Senior High School to enjoy classical music. When the Auditorium opened on the Beach, evenings of symphony or Opera hit a high note of pleasure in the community.

Emerson Buckley served as resident conductor for the Greater Miami Opera Guild for thirty-five years. His debut with the Opera, the twin bill of "I Pagliacci" and "The Secret of Suzanne," marked the first time the company featured an all-Metropolitan Opera cast. A guiding force, bringing experience from The New York City Opera and from WOR radio in New York, Buckley was ultimately appointed Artistic Director of the Company in 1973.

Western Union Telegram

To Mayor Kenneth Oka — 6/4 1957
Street and No. 136 Collins Ave. c/o Picciolo's Restaurant
Care of or Apt. No. Miami Beach

Dot - Dot - Dot - DAAH!!

Miami Beach Civic Orchestra

Opposite:
Backstage at the Miami Beach Auditorium after a 1962 performance of the love story *Turandot*, one of Giacomo Puccini's best loved operas.

From left to right, Emerson Buckley, artistic director and conductor of the Greater Miami Opera; Birgit Nilsson resplendent as the Chinese princess whose hand is available to the suitor who solves three riddles; Kenneth Oka; and Flaviano Labo.

Above:
Musical congratulations delivered to a popular Italian open-air restaurant on South Beach when Kenneth Oka was elected mayor for the first term. The Okas were hosting a celebration party with spaghetti and chianti.

179

Left Miami a Legacy

Roses for a Diva
Dr. Arturo di Filippi,
Renata Tebaldi, and
Mayor Oka following a
1961 production of the
tragic love story *André
Chenier* by Umberto
Giordano at the Miami
Beach Auditorium.
Mayor Oka presents a
key to the City of Miami
Beach to Diva Tebaldi.
Her knockout diamond
pinky ring sparkles as
brightly as her evening's
performance. She
appeared regularly at
the Metropolitan Opera
in New York until 1973.[3]

Dr. Arturo di Filippi presided over the Greater Miami Opera Guild for thirty-two years. He guided it from early days in church halls and high schools to the grand debut of the Opera at the opening of the Dade County Auditorium in 1951. Born of an Italian father and German mother, di Filippi made his way to the United States in 1912 as a deck hand on a freighter. He had a dramatic tenor voice, and in 1919 he was awarded a scholarship to attend The Julliard School of Music in New York. He made his stage debut in Sorrento. When he returned to the United States, di Filippi made some success singing commercials, gave concerts, and wrote opera transcriptions. Bad health forced him to leave New York for a warmer climate.

Performing in Miami in 1939, he was offered a post at the University of Miami. Di Filippi loved opera, especially the great Italian works, and decided that Miami should have an opera. He singlehandedly brought this genre to the tropics, making the yearly Opera Ball the social event of the season. A man of great personal style, colorful and flamboyant like the music he loved, Arturo di Filippi, it is said, was born to wear white tie and tails. The Maestro didn't forget the young people in his community, and once serenaded Dade County Commissioners to convince them to appropriate funds for school opera performances. He left an additional legacy in the renovated rehearsal hall and office building on Coral Way in Coral Gables.

Season after Season

The world's greatest performers sang their signature roles season after season. Miami Beach was such a magnet that it drew all the great names in performing arts. Joan Sutherland brought Luciano Pavarotti to sing with her in Miami before her debut at the Metropolitan Opera in New York.

1953 Regina Resnik,
Mascagni's *Cavalleria Rusticana*
1954 Licia Albanese,
Puccini's *Madame Butterfly*
1955 Nicola Moscona,
Rossini's *The Barber of Seville*
1956 Jan Peerce, Puccini's *La Bohème*
1957 Cesare Siepi, Gounod's *Faust*
1958 Dorothy Kirstein, Puccini's *Tosca*
1959 Richard Tucker,
Verdi's *Un Ballo in Maschera*
1960 Eileen Farrell,
Ponchieli's *La Gioconda*
1961 Renata Tebaldi,
Giordano's *André Chénier*
1962 Birgit Nilsson, Puccini's *Turandot*
1963 Anna Moffo, Massenet's *Manon*

Citation for
the Composer
Mayor Kenneth Oka greets three generations of Bernsteins at Miami International Airport shortly after their KLM flight arrived. He presents American conductor/composer Leonard Bernstein with a proclamation designating the week of February 17 to 28, 1963 as "New York Philharmonic Week."

Bernstein had become the first American-born music director of the New York Philharmonic five years previously. As an interpreter of music and a performer, Bernstein was magnetic and charismatic. A year later, on May 6, 1964, Bernstein made his Metropolitan Opera debut, conducting *Falstaff*. He was an active world-renowned conductor and composer until his death in 1990.

Walk, Don't Run

Newsweek, April 23, 1962[4]
Next to the compulsive chatterer and the chronic cougher, the most trying pest in the concert hall is the boor who sprints for the exit at the first hint that the music is ending. Some weeks ago in Miami Beach, Metropolitan Opera tenor Jan Peerce had hardly finished the last notes of his program, let alone begun his encores, when a third of the audience rose and bolted. "Look," the singer called to the departing backs. "I'm sure the buses are running all night!"

That Peerce should have reached his boiling point in Miami Beach was no surprise. Although loutish concert manners (as Peerce himself points out) are to be found in Carnegie Hall and all over the nation, the Miami area has a peculiarly infamous reputation among musicians. Last week— in an effort to introduce civility to Florida's Gold Coast concert goers—both the Miami Beach Community Concert Association and the Miami Civic Music Association were treating their subscribers to a combination of cajolery and threat.

Just before the duo-piano team of Vronsky and Babin returned to the stage to play encores for Civic's final concert, president Charles H. Crandon came out to announce a strict new policy: Next year, he said, all subscribers must pledge "to keep their backsides in the seats until the concert's all over—including encores." The penalty for not signing, he said, would be loss of membership; cheaters who sign and then renege would be relieved of their season tickets for eight concerts and refunded their $10.

Despite the splendid example of Jan Peerce, Miami Beach has decided not to scold its subscribers. Instead it is trying the soft sell. Last week, before pianist Leonard Pennario came onstage for Community's final concert of the season, president Kenneth Oka made a speech which flatteringly assumed that the audience would show its innate good concert manners. The result, as reported in the Miami *Herald*: "About the usual percentage of Mr. Oka's audience rose and fled on the last note of the last scheduled piece. Mr. Pennario got in his two encores by dint of waiting for a resumption of silence each time."

Great Pianist

Gina Bachauer was one of the great pianists of the twentieth century. Her mentor was Sergei Rachmaninoff, and Bachauer typified the nineteenth-century romantic piano tradition. She possessed the rigorous discipline and focus required to succeed as a concert soloist, and performed more than one hundred concerts annually.

Alec Sherman, Bachauer's husband and the conductor of the New London Orchestra, was her manager. In later years, Sherman sacrificed his own ambitions to concentrate on his wife's talents. He preserved her correspondence, press, and programs, all too often discarded or lost in the life of an active performing artist, as well as scores she had annotated, itineraries of major concert tours, and unreleased recordings.

When Sherman died in 1992, sixteen years after the death of his wife, the material was donated to Brigham Young University, where Bachauer had given some of the best performances of her career. This gift serves as a unique resource for young artists. The University's Gina Bachauer International Piano Competition and Festival provides new releases that continue to dazzle.

"It is difficult to define what talent is . . . One must have it, but everything else is work, and the courage after every disappointment to start all over again."
Gina Bachauer

Symphony Club

Frances Wolfson served as President of the Symphony Club for seven dedicated years, 1953 through 1959. The club was organized to assist the University of Miami Symphony Orchestra. Members contributed valuable musical scores, instruments for the players, and underwrote extras not provided for in a university budget.

In addition, the club conducted a series of preview programs for those interested in learning more about upcoming concerts. Several balls were held to raise funds. In 1957, the price of a ticket to these black-tie affairs was $25. During the seven years of Frances Wolfson's tenure, the Symphony Club raised $204,579.[5]

A Snake in the Garden of Eden

Zorita performed her nightly act for astonished patrons of Martha Raye's original club. Throughout the years, Miami Beach had its share of bar girls, side shows, and regular strippers, but Zorita made news because she completely bared her bosoms. Evelyn West, a stripper who performed at Leon and Eddie's, had permission to bare her breast because her act had been defined as art. The difference had to do with suggestive wiggles.

Miami Beach officials didn't get excited about the situation. Mayor Kenneth Oka was quoted in the papers as saying that the state of the undress of the girls had something to do with lack of business in the clubs. Zorita was warned that a "rough act won't be tolerated on Miami Beach."[6] Police coverage of the situation also seemed scanty.

Zorita and her Famous
Snake Dance at
the Five O'Clock Club,
2002 Collins Avenue.

The Showmandisers
Building an Empire

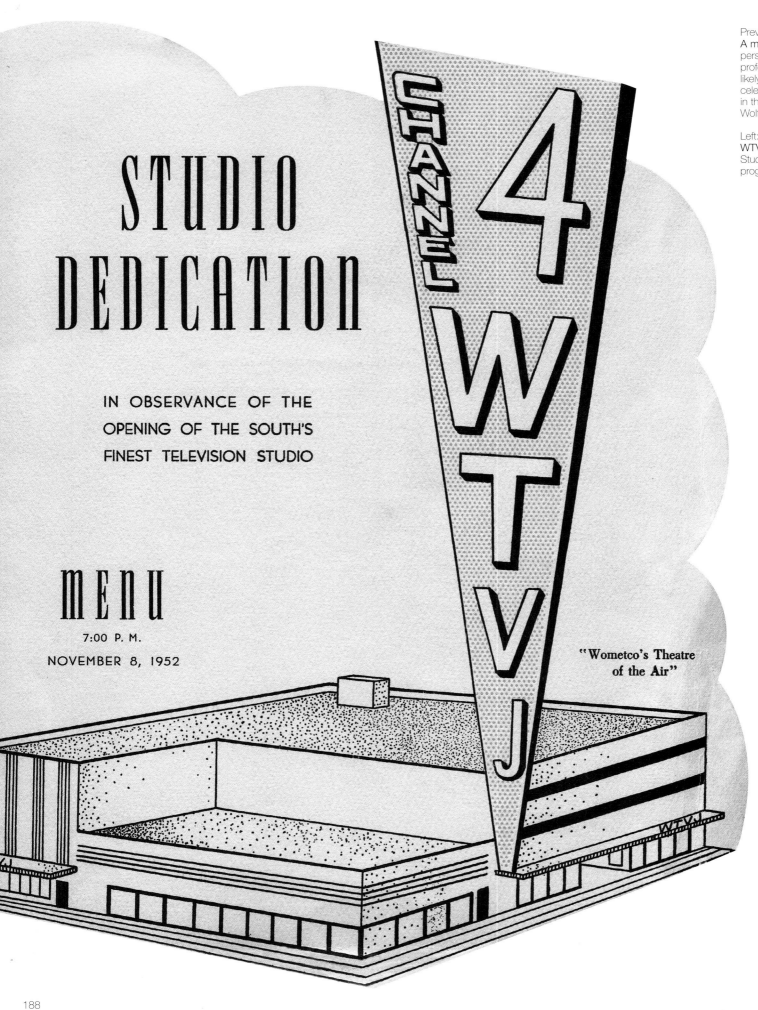

STUDIO
DEDICATION

IN OBSERVANCE OF THE
OPENING OF THE SOUTH'S
FINEST TELEVISION STUDIO

MENU

7:00 P. M.
NOVEMBER 8, 1952

CHANNEL 4 WTVJ

"Wometco's Theatre
of the Air"

Previous spread:
A montage, both personal and professional, most likely created to celebrate an event in the life of Mitchell Wolfson.

Left:
WTVJ Channel 4 Studio Dedication program, 1952

THE WOLFSONIAN FOUNDATION

1001 Washington Avenue
Miami Beach, Florida 33139
(305) 531-1001
Telex: 9102504230
U.S.A.

Castello Mackenzie-Wolfson
Casella Postale: 1367
16122 Genova
Uffici:
Via Roccatagliata Ceccardi, 1
16121 Genova
(010) 564916–17–18
Italia

Dear Michele,

Miami Beach was indeed the high rent district. A
tradition of showmanship, an endowment of extravagance
and youth gave advertising a boost toward the romantic
and outrageous. What a claque of hawkers! From the
more urbane (our dear fathers, of course) to the
smile-and-a-shoeshine yokel, selling was the common
bond. Miami Beach generated a whole industry of
persuasion. The public was as easily lured into buying
a lot as a ten-day holiday.

While our forebears expected returns on their invest-
ments, somehow their obsessive devotion to business
never resulted in self-righteous arrogance. Innocence
and pragmatism: Did the combination make most of them
free-wheeling spirits whose counterparts we see today?
What else accounts for the non-judgmental attitude
that still gives Miami Beach its nicest human flavor?

Micky

How to Build an Empire

The new Miami Theatre, built in 1947, was to be Wometco's post-war Showplace of the Americas. Demolition of existing shops on Flagler Street to make way for the building of the Miami Theatre became an event in itself.

Opposite:
Great publicity was generated when Beauty, Inc. was invited to demolish the plate glass and make way for a new theater. The professional posers arrived for the stunt in appropriate costume. Shorts and culottes allowed shapely legs to be seen, a ploy guaranteed to increase the crowd of spectators.

Left:
Ammunition, the ripe seeds of the coconut palm, was gathered at the site.
Photos c. 1946

Ready, Aim, Fire

When the signal was given and the crowd of viewers (including men still in uniform) assembled, the girls let loose and controlled chaos reigned. Duly recorded on film, the event was somewhat of a novelty in the dark ages before the television screen lit up.

Building an Empire

Wometco Enterprises, Inc. was born during the great Florida land boom of the 1920s. The company bridged a vast span of interests, all serving the public's leisure time needs. Wometco ranged from its original string of movie theaters to television stations, soft drink bottling plants, automatic vending and food service companies, film production enterprises, and the world famous Miami Seaquarium. In 1959, Wometco moved from a privately owned firm to a public corporation. In addition to his Wometco interests, Mitchell Wolfson was Chairman of the Board of the Miami Beach Federal Savings and Loan Association and Director of the First National Bank of Miami. He was also founder and served as chairman of the Miami Off-Street Parking Authority, an agency which still manages the Gusman Cultural Center in downtown Miami.

Bursting on the scene in 1925, Wometco already owned two dozen urban movie palaces in South Florida. The momentum of construction and acquisition would continue for thirty years. In 1958, when movie-going audiences were at their peak, Wometco owned thirty-one theaters, including suburban drive-ins. Starting with *Showboat* in 1929, over fifty World Premieres had been held in Miami and the Beach by the Wometco chain. W.C. Fields appeared in person at the *Showboat* premiere, and Wometco continued to use major Hollywood stars to help push its product. Nor did the company frown upon gimmicks to promote business.

Wometco needed two pictures a week to operate the theaters successfully, and there weren't yet enough to supply the new movie palaces. Once a week Wometco paid $1,000 and received all of the Fox features—fifty-two of them, one for each week—which were produced with shorts and news reels. Wometco went to Universal Films, and in order to get a five year franchise and acquire sufficient product, gave away half interest in the operating company of the Capitol Theatre. Mitchell Wolfson recalled that it was tough to pay $52,000 a year to Fox at that time. He decided that, since he had already paid for the use of the films, he would acquire some additional theaters and bought the Biltmore. There was also plenty of competition from American Broadcasting, Paramount, and other chains and independents. The struggle to make a livelihood out of the new motion picture industry and to build a chain of theaters which would provide the capitol to pay movie distributors became Wometco's first long-range goal.

Mitchell Wolfson was gifted with an infallible instinct for what the public would buy to fill its free hours. Upon entering the movie business in 1925, he borrowed $112,500 to build his first theater, The Capitol, on the corner of Miami Avenue and Northwest Third Street. Wolfson dreamed of a larger company, with the Capitol as the flagship. Built along the lines of the famous amusement palace of the same name in New York, the Capitol became the prototype of a larger empire than Wolfson could have seen on the horizon in the 1920s. (The Capitol building was converted into offices and studios for WTVJ in 1952).

On Friday, June 25, 1926, the Miami *Daily News* headlined the premier performance. The motion picture industry was thirty-one years old. Already visionaries understood that art was in a new phase of development, and this time art was partnered with science and technology. The first movie houses were equipped with white sheets tightly stretched as screens—and many trials and tribulations. As recently as 1906, theater owners gave away whole packs of tickets and saw them trampled in the street, for people were afraid to go into the movie houses. Fear of fire was part of the zeitgeist during the infancy of the industry. The first projection machines were crude affairs, and the development of fireproof magazines for reels, with fire shutters, was yet to come. Ultimately, projection equipment was enclosed in fireproof booths. The construction included reinforced concrete, tile, and stone. No wood was used, not even for baseboards or staircaps. The materials were selected to be fireproof. The Miami *Daily News* article assured a new Miami audience that the Capitol was fireproof.

MICKEY MOUSE CLUB

HERE IS THE OFFICIAL MICKEY MOUSE CLUB MEMBERSHIP CARD

MEMBER — **MICKEY MOUSE** — **Club**

This Certifies that

_____

is a Registered Member of the
MICKEY MOUSE CLUB

Chief Mickey Mouse

AND HERE IS THE OFFICIAL MICKEY MOUSE BUTTON

Membership Card and Button, illustrated at left, will be given Boys and Girls FREE upon presentation of Membership Application Forms properly filled out.

Get Your Membership Card and Button, Boys and Girls—They're Going to be Valuable and Helpful in Many Ways. Surprises Prize Offers, Special Rewards and Many Other Attractive Events are Being Arranged for Members in Good Standing and a Member in Good Standing is a Boy or Girl who Secures and Carries a Membership Card and Wears the Mickey Mouse Club Button at all times.

MICKEY MOUSE CLUB CREED

I will be a square shooter in my home, in school, on the playgrounds, where-ever I may be.

I will be truthful and honorable and strive, always, to make myself a better and more useful little citizen.

I will respect my elders and help the aged, the helpless and children smaller than myself.

In short, I will be a good American!—

MICKEY MOUSE CLUB

The Capitol

The Capitol was born in the era of silent movies. An orchestra opened the evening's performance with "The Star Spangled Banner." An address of welcome to the viewers was formally conducted. News events of the world were viewed on the screen while an organist played on the mighty Wurlitzer. Audience sing-alongs were part of the fun. While the organist performed in full view of the audience, the orchestra pit was recessed. The featured attraction, *The Midnight Sun*, rolled to the sounds of live orchestral music. Originally a play set in St. Petersburg, Russia, prior to the First World War, *The Midnight Sun* was adapted to the screen and featured such attractions as a large gold divan once used by Napoleon, as well as rugs valued at $20,000—a lot of money at that time. "The Ballet of Jewels" staged therein was a masterpiece of stage craft. It was shot in a reproduction of the interior of the Imperial Russian Ballet as it was at the height of its magnificence. Three months later, a devastating hurricane struck Miami, and the Capitol remained standing as one of the few undamaged buildings. Before nightfall on the day the storm hit, the theater became a Red Cross Relief Center. The materials selected to be fireproof turned out to be storm resistant as well. In the days before air conditioning adjusted the heat and humidity to a comfort zone, two sets of twin fans swept the Capitol Theatre with a breeze from Biscayne Bay. The spacious lobby was tiled with rubber in black and gold squares. The general seating capacity was almost fifteen hundred. An immense chandelier illuminated the main auditorium. Patrons luxuriated in state-of-the-art opera chairs. Miami's own Atlas Rock Company provided local materials. The 1926-27 season included *The Flaming Frontier*, the story of the battle between the Seventh Calvary and Native Americans at Little Big Horn. It was filmed on location at West Point, New York, at various Indian Camps, and ended with a real view of the battlefield in the Black Hills. The film was historically correct in every detail. Retired army officer Colonel George L. Bryam, who arrived at Little Big Horn only ten years after the battle ended and interviewed surviving Chiefs who had fought there, verified the account.

Capitol Theatre Interior
Wometco Credit Union meeting. Fourth from the left, standing, is Sonny Shepherd, manager of the Biltmore Theatre, May 1935.

Parental Umbrella
During the depression years, the Wometco Credit Union provided a parental umbrella to shield its employees from the financial gyrations of unstable times. The attendees that appear in the photograph look well attired.

The company also created the Wometco Thanksgiving Festival. For two weeks before the holiday, two people could buy admission to the theaters for the price of one ticket plus an article of food. The food stuffs requested included potatoes, canned goods, cured meats, and other non-perishable products. In this manner, Wometco fed two thousand families in the Miami area annually.

Mitchell Wolfson with Robert J. O'Donnell, chief barker of Variety Club's International, at Variety's twelfth annual convention, their right hands in the leather gloves of the straw Jai-Alai cestas, April 1948, at the Biscayne Fronton Club.

Chief Barkers

Barkers met yearly, elected officers, reported on charitable activities, and conferred an annual humanitarian award. The convention headquarters was housed at the luxurious Roney Plaza Hotel. Business meetings were confined to mornings and early afternoons, after which every sort of entertainment was made available: deep sea fishing, swimming, motor boating, yachting, golfing, night clubbing, horse racing, dog racing, Jai-Alai, and just plain loafing.

The Singing Cowboy

Gene Autry appeared in person at the Capitol Theater when the motion picture house was in its heyday. Stars from all strata of the Hollywood heavens were brought to Miami by Wometco, but the very biggest three days for youngsters occurred when Gene Autry made his personal appearances. Autry recorded "Rudolph the Red-Nosed Reindeer" in 1949, one of the biggest-selling singles of all time. He was among the top ten moneymakers in Hollywood films from 1938 to 1942. By 1942, he was making more than $600,000 a year from movies, records, a weekly radio show and personal appearances. The television version of "The Gene Autry Show" premiered in 1950 on CBS and featured 104 half-hour episodes.

Gene Autry and Miami Chief of Police Walter Headley. The Singing Cowboy was made Honorary Chief of Police.

TELEV

Comes to

PREVIEW
MIAMI THEATRE

See Television in action NOW! GRAND OPENING TODAY of live demonstrations by Television Station WTVJ and Radio Station WMIE in the beautiful Miami Theater . . . featuring TODAY and TOMORROW STEWART - WARNER sets by the HOUSE OF TELEVISION, third floor, Seybold Bldg., YOUR STEWART - WARNER TELEVISION DEALER.

WTVJ
CHANNEL 4 · MIAMI

FLORIDA'S PIONEER TELEVISION STATION

Nineteen N. W. Third St., Miami 32, Fla.

SION!
1IAMI!

USE OF TELEVISION PRESENTS
TEWART WARNER

VIDEORAMA T-711

Big, 10-inch picture tube gives you direct "front row" pictures . . . a magnificent custom-built cabinet, rich African mahogany in smooth modern design. Perfect for the Florida home. All video bands <u>and</u> standard radio reception for thrilling entertainment 'round the clock! $564.57 COMPLETE . . . includes tax, installation and 1-year guaranteed service. Terms as low as $165 down and $6.95 a week for the set. Installation and tax can also be budgeted.

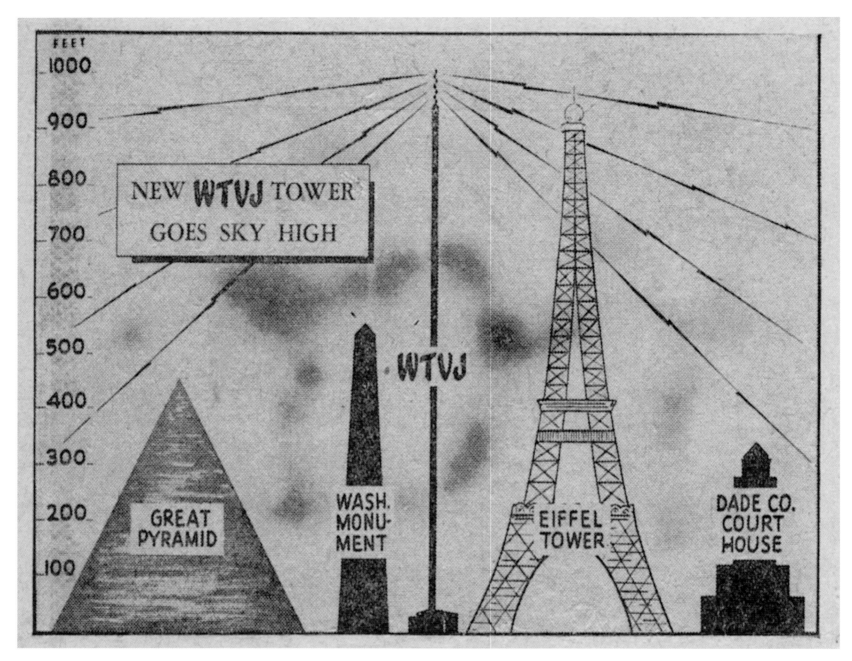

FEET
1000
900
800
700
600
500
400
300
200
100

NEW **WTVJ** TOWER GOES SKY HIGH

GREAT PYRAMID

WASH. MONU-MENT

WTVJ

EIFFEL TOWER

DADE CO. COURT HOUSE

Taller than the Eiffel Tower
The drawing above, prepared by WTVJ artists, graphically compares the station's new tower height with some of the best known tall structures locally and around the word.

The TV tower will be a few feet taller than the Eiffel Tower and nearly three times the height of Dade County's skyscraper courthouse.

The Hope of the World

Television arrived in Miami unnoticed by most Miamians. However, sharp-eyed spectators spied a lacy steel shaft topped with three wire butterflies, a 306-foot-high antenna erected in December, 1948, atop the Everglades Hotel. Speculation was that the Goodyear Blimp was relocating its mooring site to a downtown location. Miamians soon learned to call the unidentified object a "three bay antennae." It was to project the new station's programs into the homes of South Florida, and change the perception of time and space forever.

Five years later, the experiment of television was proclaimed a success, and a new tower was installed to receive and send greater capacity signals. The initial tower atop the Everglades Hotel was surpassed in power by the new transmitter 625 percent. One hundred thousand watt power was the maximum allowed by the Federal Communication Commission. The tower was fabricated in New York City by Lehigh Structural Steel Corporation and shipped to Miami in twenty-eight-foot sections. It became the tallest structure in the South and the highest ever attempted in what was known as the Florida hurricane belt. It was also the first commercial tower of comparable size to be equipped with an elevator. A round trip in the elevator took at least eighteen minutes with no stops.

The construction of this live wire required the creative resources of Miami engineering firm Jorgenson and Schreffler. They pondered how to design a thousand-foot structure capable of withstanding hurricane wind pressure. The tower, situated on a plot of ground fifteen feet above sea level, was triangular in shape and measured eight feet on each of its three sides. It weighed in at three hundred tons. The engineers came up with thirty tons of wires called "tension cables" to brace the tower. The bracing was elaborately arranged and the wonder of all who beheld it. Twenty-four main cables were attached to the tower at different levels. Two each connected with twelve reinforced concrete anchors called "dead men" placed in the ground. The "dead men" were located in concentric circles three hundred and seven hundred feet from the tower base. Each weighed three hundred and sixty thousand pounds, and all twelve contained enough concrete and reinforcing steel to build a 130-room hotel. Living quarters were provided in the air-conditioned transmitter building so that engineers could attend the tower twenty-four hours a day.

Mitchell Wolfson saw film, television, and radio as the hope of the world. He understood that the radio signal, which now included television, was capable of intercontinental travel more rapidly than the world's weapons of destruction. Home less than three years from his role in the aftermath of World War II as rebuilder of communication systems in Germany, Wolfson comprehended the need for speed. Furthermore, he intuited the significance of communications as a fundamental evolutionary step. When selling the merits of this new industry, Wolfson articulated the enormous value of having instruments by which Heads of State could immediately communicate with one other. He calculated television to be so powerful that a policy was formulated forbidding the endorsements of political candidates for office. However, he allowed endorsements on issues and took stands against gambling, both legal and illegal.

History was made in these early days. *The Arthur Godfrey Show* and *Kukla, Fran and Ollie* appeared in more than 22,000 homes served by WTVJ. News was broadcast from the very beginning, and WTVJ was the first television station in the United States to offer daily editorials. Wolfson understood that television served the community, and WTVJ's remote unit went everywhere and filmed anything worth bringing to the television audience. Filmed "on the spot," there was a shopper's guide program and a "college of musical knowledge" broadcast. The acceptance of television increased rapidly as special sports and spot programs became available.

One such great newsworthy event was the sidewalk talk by Estes Kefauver. The Kefauver committee was investigating crime in interstate commerce, and evidence that Miami was the wintertime hub of organized crime was presented before the United States Senate. The Miami citizenry was grateful for the Kefauver investigation. The city tolerated the unfavorable publicity in order to rid itself of racketeers and corruption. Kefauver subpoenaed books and records of nightclubs and hotels in Dade County. He exposed the S and G Syndicate and forced it to fold in Miami Beach. Members were brought to trial. In 1952, as the Wometco building was opening, Kefauver returned to Miami during his campaign for United States President. He lost to Adlai E. Stevenson, who in turn lost to General Dwight D. Eisenhower. This local and in-studio programming did much to increase the number of viewers. In the fall of 1949, WTVJ risked its valuable cameras and indispensable crew to produce the world's first live telecast of a hurricane.

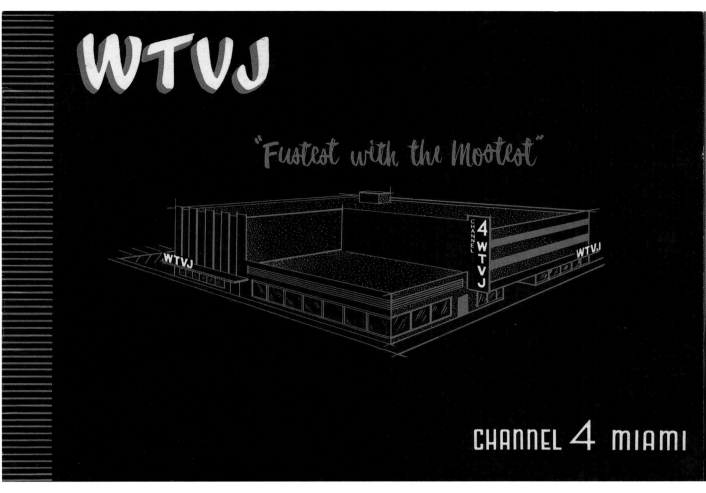

WTVJ

"Fustest with the Mostest"

CHANNEL 4 MIAMI

Left:
Actual footage from Wometco archive of first hurricane ever broadcast, 1949.

Opposite:
America's First Station for TV News. Television studios and general offices of WTVJ Channel 4. Excellent newscaster Ralph Renick helps Wometco make history.

The First with the Most

First Mickey Mouse Club started at the Biltmore Theatre, 1931

First Midnight Movies at the Capitol

First foreign art films shown in the nation at the Mayfair. Laurence Olivier's *Hamlet*—one of the first of the firsts—was a smash hit.

First escalator in a movie theater at the Carib, $78,000

First Florida TV station, WTVJ

First live telecast of a hurricane, 1949

First telecast from a blimp, January 2, 1950—Orange Bowl: Santa Clara 21, Kentucky 13

First nationally broadcast, regularly scheduled TV editorial with Ralph Renick, 1957

Largest TV Plant in the South

Architect A. Herbert Mathes, A.I.A. Occupying the site and structure of Louis Wolfson's East Coast Jobbing House, backing up to the site of the former Capitol Theatre. Converted in time for the gala introduction of television to the State of Florida, Monday, March 21, 1949, the flagship Capitol Theatre became Wometco's Theatre of the Air. The studio had practiced sending test patterns on the TV airwaves since mid-February, and had successfully reached the Palm Beach area eighty miles north of Miami. A specially built television truck was purchased. The filming of news and special events was anticipated. At this moment, Paris, France, owned three hundred television sets. Russia was conducting extensive research; Britain was producing daily programming and an appreciable number of people owned sets. But the United States led the world in television ownership.

WTVJ Studio A
The programming
console and control
room at Studio A were
photographed for an
elegant brochure
published in conjunction
with the opening of
the new home
and extensive facilities
of WTVJ Channel 4.
Using sophisticated
graphics, the brochure
laid out the wonders of
the new frontier of
television production
and programming for
potential clients.

The brochure featured
WTVJ's eleven film
remote and studio
cameras, as well as a
peek into the future:
a development and
research laboratory.
Seven thousand square
feet in size, Studio A
was the pride of the
plant. Everything was
rigged to provide
precise centralized
operation. A multitude
of lights were hung
and strung, to illuminate
live broadcasts with
studio audiences.

Lighting control centers
with Kliegl rotary
switch systems offered
the latest technology.
Remote control
consoles operated
electronic dimmers,
and bases were
specifically designed
for studio cameras and
microphone usage.

The First Year of Television

A published report after the first full year of operation of
the WTVJ transmitter presented an enviable record.
Two thousand, seven hundred and thirty hours had been
accumulated "on air." Program loss due to transmitter
failure during the first year was only "two hours and sixty-
five minutes."[1] But the real loss was to Wometco. It took
time before there were sufficient television sets for
advertisers to buy enough time at WTVJ to pay for the
cost of programming. The company incurred heavy
financial losses during that first year. The prices of television
sets dropped as the demand increased. A year later there
were four million in the United States. They were fed by
102 stations in fifty-nine cities.

Color television was predicted but appeared to be in the distant future. Still, there were days when faith in the talking box wavered. Wolfson understood that the confusion and uncertainty would lift over time, and knew that Wometco would eventually benefit in great measure from the new technology. When he built the studio in 1949, Wolfson had never even seen a TV set or watched a TV program. But he had heard about it. Within a decade, television operations in Miami were responsible for most of the net income of Wometco Enterprises. During the halcyon days of television, sets were demonstrated with live broadcasts at retailers.

Introduction of the television set into homes prompted newspaper articles recalling the days when room was made in the living room for a new fangled gadget called "radio." The first television sets produced were floor models encased in wooden frames with traditional features: Colonial, Queen Anne, French Provincial, and Moderne styles. Living rooms were rearranged, and television parties were thrown when sets were brought home. The dinner hour ended earlier, for no one wanted to miss a single portion of the evening's programming. More newspaper articles reassured the public that watching television would not injure their eyes. And the great debate about the effect of television on the mind of the viewing public was born.

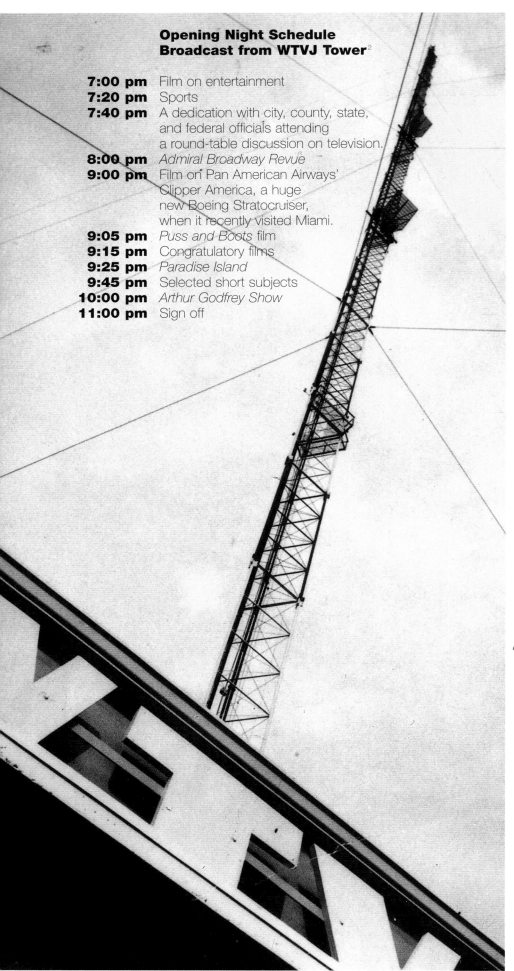

Opening Night Schedule
Broadcast from WTVJ Tower[2]

7:00 pm	Film on entertainment
7:20 pm	Sports
7:40 pm	A dedication with city, county, state, and federal officials attending a round-table discussion on television.
8:00 pm	*Admiral Broadway Revue*
9:00 pm	Film on Pan American Airways' Clipper America, a huge new Boeing Stratocruiser, when it recently visited Miami.
9:05 pm	*Puss and Boots* film
9:15 pm	Congratulatory films
9:25 pm	*Paradise Island*
9:45 pm	Selected short subjects
10:00 pm	*Arthur Godfrey Show*
11:00 pm	Sign off

WTVJ Goes on the Air

Opening night, March 21, 1949, WTVJ telecasted for four hours and maintained this schedule for the first few weeks of operation. Miami had almost a thousand TV sets waiting to be initiated. These were owned, for the most part, by bars, appliance stores, and big spenders who always bought the status symbol of the moment. People stood four deep at store windows watching the picture move foggily across the screen. When 1950 rolled around, Channel 4 maintained a 48-hour week.

In what was to become a significant move, Channel 4 decided to broadcast the January 2, 1950 Orange Bowl Game between Kentucky and Santa Clara. Miami now counted 17,000 television set owners. Channel 4 was soaring, literally and figuratively. It produced the world's first telecast from a blimp. The next year, the tide turned dramatically, and television left its novelty status, becoming firmly entrenched in the hearts and homes of the American public. Life at home has never been the same since.
The hour long *Arthur Godfrey Show* was the feature of the opening night program. The station acquired the popular show by special contract with Columbia Broadcasting System, and it became a regular weekly program.
The Admiral Broadway Revue, also a Columbia production, was a variety show, and one of the first television productions "on the waves." Both Godfrey and the Admiral Show were shipped to Miami on film from New York.

William S. Paley, the brains and energy behind CBS, wrote a short article asserting television's obligation to develop its potential as a source of public information. Like Mitchell Wolfson, Paley foresaw television's immense power on the final tallies of ballot box elections. Television achieved an unprecedented intimacy between speaker and listeners, and between program and audience. The addition of sight to sound introduced the challenge of viewer inspection of entertainers, personalities, salesmen, politicians, products, premises, and promises.

"The assumption of such a self-imposed task entails a great responsibility for every broadcaster. His public will increasingly shape its opinions by what is seen and heard on television . . . the public must be kept fully informed if we are to achieve the still remote blueprints of a democratic peace and equal opportunities for the pursuit of happiness."
William Paley[3]

The Ticker Symbol is WOM

Ten years after opening night, on Thursday May 7, 1959, the Wolfson family distributed Class A Stock to employees at the price of $10.00 per share. This offering came less than a week after Wometco became a public stock company. 290,000 shares of Wometco Class A common stock were offered at $10.75 per share. Six years later, Wometco Enterprises was listed on the New York Stock Exchange with the ticket symbol WOM.

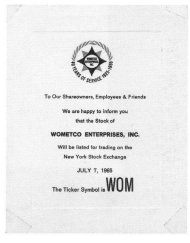

To Our Shareowners, Employees & Friends

We are happy to inform you
that the Stock of

WOMETCO ENTERPRISES, INC.

Will be listed for trading on the
New York Stock Exchange

JULY 7, 1965

The Ticker Symbol is **WOM**

Mitchell Wolfson with showmandiser par excellance Ed Sullivan, pioneer host of upscale vaudeville of the waves.

"a really, really big shew. . ."
Ed Sullivan

Great Stone Face

Ed Sullivan arrived with the birth of television and became a twenty-three-year TV institution. The first telecast was on a Sunday night, and featured comic team Dean Martin and Jerry Lewis. Affectionately known as "The Great Stone Face," Sullivan had cardinal moments of infamy including the introduction of Elvis Presley and his rotating hips to a newly established adolescent audience, and the presentation of Britain's Beatles to America in 1964. The viewing world at home was riveted to the screen as the Beatles appeared in the Napoleon Room at Miami Beach's Deauville Hotel for their American debut.

In a more serious vein, many sociologists claim that Ed Sullivan did more to ease the chill of the Cold War than any politician. He produced a warm persona of Soviet Russia for the American public via the air waves, using the Bolshoi and the Moseyev Ballets and the Moscow Circus. At times he could be said to have truly brought a tiny ray of light in an otherwise dark postwar period.

The Honeymooner

Jackie Gleason was a leading personality of American television. The round, jovial Gleason had his own hour-long variety program, *The Jackie Gleason Show*, on and off during the 1950s and 60s. On this show, he created and developed memorable characters, especially bus driver Ralph Kramden. Ralph became the central blustering character in *The Honeymooners* (1952-57), a comedy series that over the years achieved and has maintained the status of a classic. The thirty-nine episodes of this show have been in syndication since their original run ended.

In later years, he made Miami Beach his home. He was another star of the CBS entertainment heaven. *The Jackie Gleason Show* originated at the Miami Beach Auditorium. At any given moment, Bing Crosby, Liberace, or Alan King was in Miami Beach to do a Gleason TV show. After his death in 1987, the auditorium was renamed the Jackie Gleason Center of Performing Arts. He is remembered by the trademark phrase, "Away we go!"

Public relations wizard Hank Meyer, Jackie Gleason, Jack Philbin and Mitchell Wolfson, left to right.

"How sweet it is"
Jackie Gleason

"Imagine an Irishman made king of Miami Beach; that's like making Arthur Goldberg Pope."
Bob Hope to Miami *Herald* columnist Hy Gardner[a]

A note from Joan Crawford to Mitchell Wolfson articulates her delight upon receiving a typical Florida Fruit Basket.

The Florida Fruit Basket has been nourishing Americans and promoting the virtues of the Sunshine State for over a hundred years. The Wolfsons sent so many baskets to friends and clients throughout the years that it was a logical step to acquire a piece of the business. When Miss Crawford thanked the Wolfsons for the sea grape jelly, she was referring to a pleasure that is uniquely Floridian in the continental United States.

Sea grapes *(Coccolobis Uvifera)* have grown wild in warmer coastal areas all over the world. They are one of the native trees of Florida and quite comfortable in the coastal hammock culture. The round leathery leaves are distinctive, and sometimes feature prominent red veins. The fruits ripen all year round and are enjoyed by people and birds alike. While birds devour them on site, humans prepare wine or jelly. In recent years, the Rare Fruit Council has extended the audience and scope of the sea grape with the addition of sea grape soup and sea grape juice for a new generation of connoisseurs.

HOTEL **Fontainebleau**

MIAMI BEACH, FLORIDA

November 11, 1955

Dear Mitchell,

Thank you so much for the beautiful yellow and orange chrysanthemums and the large basket of fruit, "pecan delights", honey, nuts, mint almonds, sea grape jelly, "Becco" candies and cocoanut patties. You sent so much and I'm so grateful to you.

I hope I'll be able to come back to Miami soon, when I'll have more time to become better acquainted with you all, as you are so hospitable and friendly.

Sincerely,

JOAN CRAWFORD

Mitchell Wolfson
306 N. Miami Ave.
Miami, Fla.

Recipe for Sea Grape Jelly

Spread a sheet under a sea grape tree and shake the branches. Clusters of fruit do not evenly ripen so this method allows the fruit that is ready to dislodge itself without being pulled or roughed up. Using only fruit that is a deep purple with soft skin, wash Sea grapes and put into a large pot. Cover with water and boil for thirty minutes.

Drain juice off the sea grapes and strain. Measure one cup of juice to one cup sugar, return to the stove and continue boiling rapidly until it starts to pop. Then pour into hot containers and seal. The jelly is a brilliant light amethyst in color and the taste is a tropical treat, slightly salty.

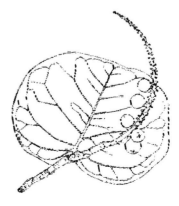

Female on the Beach

Photographed in Nassau, Bahamas, Miss Joan Crawford, with Mitchell Wolfson on her right and Harry Hambleton on her left, cuts the symbolic ribbon to formally open the Caribbean Bottling Company's new plant in 1962. Three years later it was running at a capacity of over one million cases yearly. The opening of the Caribbean Bottling Company was telecast on WTVJ Miami and in Nassau. Children presenting Pepsi-Cola bottle tops could gain entrance to see *Female on the Beach*, a movie starring Miss Crawford.

The telecast must have caused quite a stir among the Miami cognoscenti, as Wometco owned far-flung Coca-Cola bottling operations. The secret here was that foreign investors were stymied from owning outright interests in the Bahamas. Through Crawford and circuitous routes, Wolfson ended up in the Pepsi bottling business.

Agricultural Showplace

For a brief moment, Florida's famous Citrus Tower, perched on the highest observation point in the State of Florida, was aggregate in the consolidation of the Wometco empire. After going public in 1959, Wometco aggressively acquired tourist attractions in the United States and abroad. The Citrus Tower, showplace for the agricultural empire in the center of the State, Flipper's Sea School, and the Conch Tour Trains of Key West joined Wometco's enterprising entertainment industry.

The high land of central Florida, one hundred miles long down the center of the state, is sometimes called the "Ridge Section." It is blessed with the cool nights necessary to bring out the true sweetness and color of citrus fruit. These conditions allow for the most intense concentration of citrus in the world.

The two hundred foot tower was built at Clermont (regarded as "the gem of the hills") as a monumental tribute to Florida's Citrus Industry. An orange crowned the tower at 540 feet above sea level. The tower was reinforced by steel and, according to local lore, generous portions of vitamin C. The tower was functional as well as symbolic. It contained a major packing plant. Gift boxes were packed and shipped to the eastern and middle states of the country. In the 1960s, Florida produced over 80% of the nation's citrus fruit and a third of the entire world's citrus crop. One seedling orange tree could yield thirty boxes of fruit. A visitor to the tower could carry oranges back in bags.

A citrus calendar was published that contained seasonal information. Navel oranges were ready between mid-November and mid-January. Florida tangelos were ripe from mid-November to Valentine's Day, and temple oranges could be eaten in February, lasting only five weeks. The famous pink grapefruit season began in mid-November and stretched seven months to the first of June. Valencia oranges had a short season which lasted as long as spring. The Florida Citrus Tower represented the State at the 1964 New York World's Fair.

The Florida Citrus Tower represented the state at the 1964 New York World's Fair.

Recipe for Marmalade

**Two oranges
Two lemons
Sugar
Water**

First slice fruit as thinly as possible, saving seeds. After slicing fruit, measure it carefully, and add exactly as much water as fruit. Pour water over fruit, and let stand forty-eight hours. Then bring to boil and boil for an hour. Boil seeds up in water. Strain them out, and add water in which they cooked to fruit. The seeds contain the pectin which causes the jelling process. After boiling, let it stand over night. Next day boil again, but add equal amount of sugar as you have fruit and water. Boil until it thickens to your fancy. Stir several times while it is standing, so each piece of fruit has an equal chance to soften.

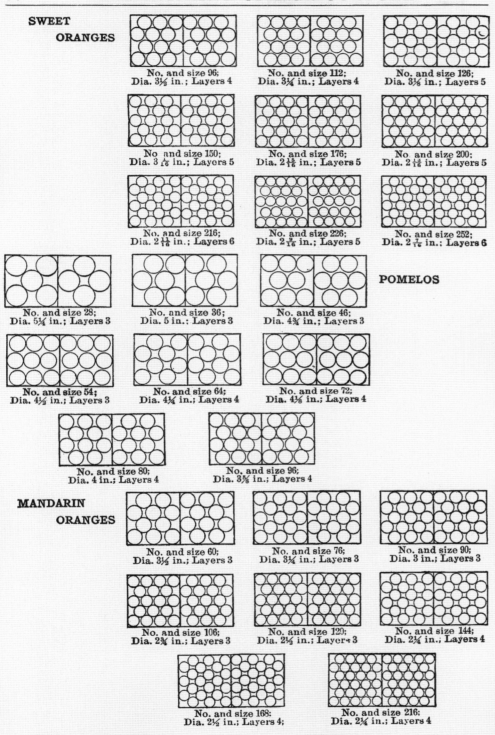

SWEET ORANGES

No. and size 96; Dia. 3½ in.; Layers 4
No. and size 112; Dia. 3¼ in.; Layers 4
No. and size 126; Dia. 3⅛ in.; Layers 5

No and size 150; Dia. 3 1/16 in.; Layers 5
No. and size 176; Dia. 2 14/16 in.; Layers 5
No. and size 200; Dia. 2 13/16 in.; Layers 5

No. and size 216; Dia. 2 11/16 in.; Layers 6
No. and size 226; Dia. 2 9/16 in.; Layers 5
No. and size 252; Dia. 2 7/16 in.; Layers 6

No. and size 28; Dia. 5¼ in.; Layers 3
No. and size 36; Dia. 5 in.; Layers 3
No. and size 46; Dia. 4¾ in.; Layers 3

POMELOS

No. and size 54; Dia. 4½ in.; Layers 3
No. and size 64; Dia. 4¼ in.; Layers 4
No. and size 72; Dia. 4⅛ in.; Layers 4

No. and size 80; Dia. 4 in.; Layers 4
No. and size 96; Dia. 3⅝ in.; Layers 4

MANDARIN ORANGES

No. and size 60; Dia. 3½ in.; Layers 3
No. and size 76; Dia. 3¼ in.; Layers 3
No. and size 90; Dia. 3 in.; Layers 3

No. and size 106; Dia. 2¾ in.; Layers 3
No. and size 120; Dia. 2½ in.; Layers 3
No. and size 144; Dia. 2¼ in.; Layers 4

No. and size 168; Dia. 2½ in.; Layers 4;
No. and size 216; Dia. 2¼ in.; Layers 4

Fig. 20.—Method of Packing Various sizes of Citrus Fruits. From Cultivation of Citrus Fruits, by H. H. Hume.
—By Permission of The Macmillan Company.

Blueprint for Marketing Citrus Fruits

Record yields of citrus crops have been recorded since the growing season of 1884-85. 600,000 boxes were packed that year. By the time of the land boom in Miami, 16,600,000 boxes valued at $30,000,000 were packed and shipped throughout the country. The industry itself dates back another hundred years to 1773, when orange groves already dotted the fertile lands flanking the St. Johns River from Jacksonville as far south as Deland, Florida.[6]

Citrus trees in Florida like sandy soil, hammock soil, and muck soil, as long as the land has been drained. The Lake district in Florida affords a certain amount of protection from the cold. After a trial and error life cycle, Florida growers settled in this section of the State. Although it usually takes five years to bring a grove to bearing age, a grove is considered mature after eight to ten years and requires constant attention. The yield of citrus trees per acre varies as much as the yield of corn. Mature trees should produce two hundred boxes of fruit per acre. Citrus fruit is harvested with clippers. Picking is usually paid for per box, and packing is state-of-the-art.

There is more to packing a box of citrus fruit than merely putting oranges or grapefruits into a crate. Fruit is first dried and polished for the sake of appearance. Then it is sized, wrapped, and packed. In packing, it is critical that fruits keep their original positions in the box. Although well adapted to long shipments, loose fruits can bruise in transit, resulting in a loss in market value.

The State of Florida has packing houses and independent shippers throughout the Citrus Belt. The Florida Citrus Exchange has functioned since 1909. Headquartered in Tampa, the Exchange handled one third of the citrus crop. The rest of the growers remained independent until 1928, when they formed the Florida Citrus Growers Clearing House Associated at Winter Haven; practically all of the independent growers joined. The clearing house helped the growers pack more efficiently, promoted wider distribution of the volume of Florida citrus fruits by advertising, and established equitable freight rates.

The marketing of citrus fruits begins as early as mid-September. Between two and eight percent of the crop is shipped in October, mostly by rail. Sixty percent goes to market during the winter months of November through February, bringing minerals, vitamins, energy, and sunshine to grimmer winter climes.[7]

"Besides a full assortment of vitamins A, B, C, D, and E, powerful nerve tonics, these oranges all contain notable amounts of actual tissue-building nourishment."[8]

Greatest Marine Aquarium

In 1960, the Miami Seaquarium was acquired by Wometco Enterprises. Rated one of the state's five most popular tourist attractions, Seaquarium occupied a little more than fifty acres on Virginia Key. When it opened, water was collected from each of the seven seas and poured into the main tank. This gesture was intended to symbolize the world-wide importance of opening the greatest marine aquarium in existence. Wometco added an ultramodern monorail, and appropriately christened the first official car with water from the main tank to establish continuity.

Previous spread:
Landscaping Virginia Key for the new Seaquarium

Left:
Construction of the main tank at the Miami Seaquarium, 1954
Within the cast concrete shell, one can see the two-tiered viewing windows and the instant landscaping set into place.

Below:
Jinks, a sea lion, balances a plastic ball for a 1961 annual meeting of Wometco Enterprise, Inc. *Business Week* featured Jinks and Pinky the Penguin with a copy of the annual report under her flipper in a feature on company management. It was reported in the local press that after Jinks dropped the Wometco ball, he applauded his own display of balancing skill. The stockholders' annual event was dubbed "a meeting with a porpoise."[9]

Caribbean Eden
Tropical Movie Palace

Wometco Theater
Miami Beach · Florida
Theater.

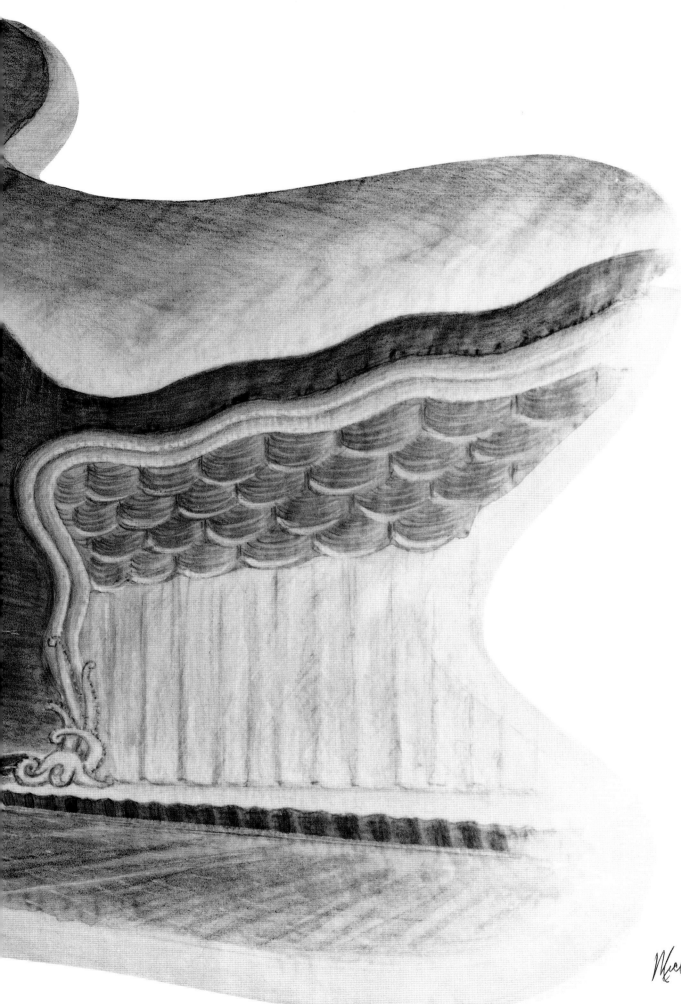

Michael J. De Angelis
architect
1950

The Tropical Carib:
A Most Exciting and Modern Theatre

The Carib Theater on Lincoln Road, designed to be one of the most exciting and modern theaters in the world, opened on December 22, 1950. Filled with a palette of rich color and themes of the tropical splendors of Caribbean countries, the Carib was the result of Wometco's mission to built a theater with an exterior and interior that could conform to South Florida's climactic conditions and reflect the natural and cultural richness of the sub-tropical region. After conducting a national competition, Mitchell Wolfson hired architect Michael J. DeAngelis to create a state-of-the-art facility which, as a result of planning and ingenuity, became the last word in the integration of site with structure.

The moviegoer was greeted by a remarkable thirty by thirty-five foot mural, a pictorial relief map of the Caribbean sea region extending north to Southern Florida and including portions of Mexico and South America, all of the Bahamas, and the Greater and Lesser Antilles. A large directional star served as a compass. The facade was porcelain enameled steel, illuminated at night by dramatic flood lights placed atop the Plexiglas marquee. The three-dimensional lettering was animated neon lighting spelling out the name of the theater with a ruby red chasing effect on a coral colored background. The alternately flashing white neon tubing on the letters made this a show stopper of an entrance. The Carib was an unusual combination of architecture, artistry, and technology.

A sense of the movement and drama of the sea were carried throughout the decorative scheme. The marquee's wavy lines indicate the roll of the sea and the wave motif is carried directly into the auditorium. The flora and fauna of Central America were also inspirations. Plexiglas birds, fountains, miniature waterfalls, pools, and plantings were used to reinforce the thematic scheme. At night, varied colored lights were used to change effects.

From the Fertile Tropics,
A Goddess of
Fruits and Flowers

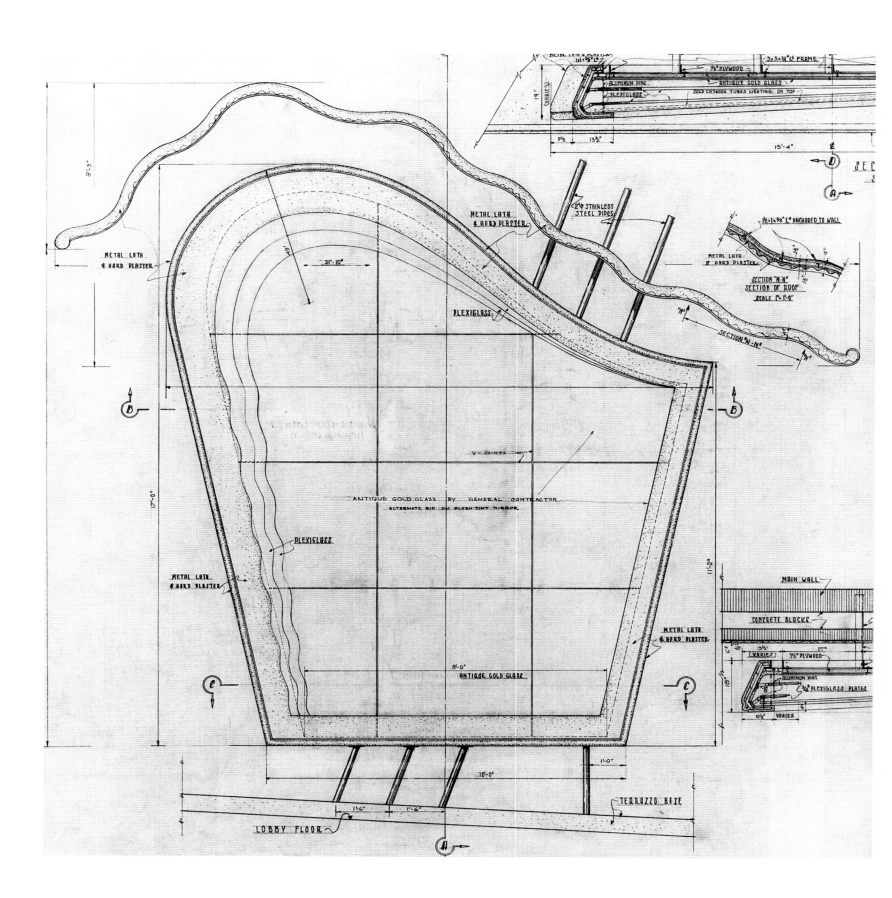

METAL LATH & PLASTER

1½ PLYWOOD

3x3x⅛" L.S FRAME

ALUMINUM PINS

ANTIQUE GOLD GLASS

PLEXIGLASS

COLD CATHODE TUBES LIGHTING ON TOP

19" (VARIES)

7½" 13½"

15'-4"

8'-3"

METAL LATH & HARD PLASTER

21'-10"

METAL LATH & HARD PLASTER

2"ⱷ STAINLESS STEEL PIPES

1½ x 1 x ⅜" L.S ANCHORED TO WALL

METAL LATH & HARD PLASTER

SECTION "N-N"
SECTION OF ROOF
SCALE 1"= 1'-0"

PLEXIGLASS

SECTION "N-N"

17'-0"

V - JOINTS

ANTIQUE GOLD GLASS BY GENERAL CONTRACTOR

ALTERNATE BID ON FLESH TINT MIRROR

11'-2"

MAIN WALL

CONCRETE BLOCKS

PLEXIGLASS

METAL LATH & HARD PLASTER

METAL LATH & HARD PLASTER

8'-0"
ANTIQUE GOLD GLASS

13½" (VARIES) 27" 1½" PLYWOOD

18"

ALUMINUM PINS

¾" PLEXIGLASS PLATES

10½" VARIES

1'-0"

10'-0"

TERRAZZO BASE

1'-6" 1'-6"

LOBBY FLOOR

A

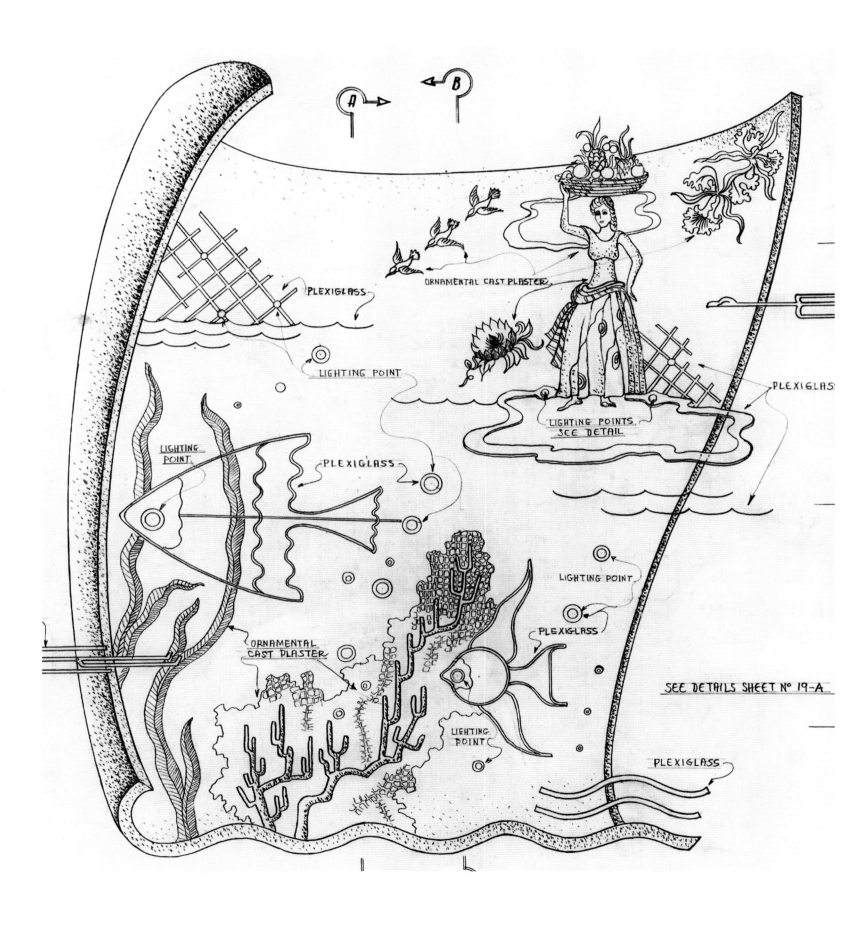

PLEXIGLASS

LIGHTING POINT

LIGHTING POINT

PLEXIGLASS

ORNAMENTAL CAST PLASTER

LIGHTING POINTS SEE DETAIL

ORNAMENTAL CAST PLASTER

PLEXIGLASS

LIGHTING POINT

PLEXIGLASS

LIGHTING POINT

SEE DETAILS SHEET Nº 19-A

PLEXIGLASS

A

B

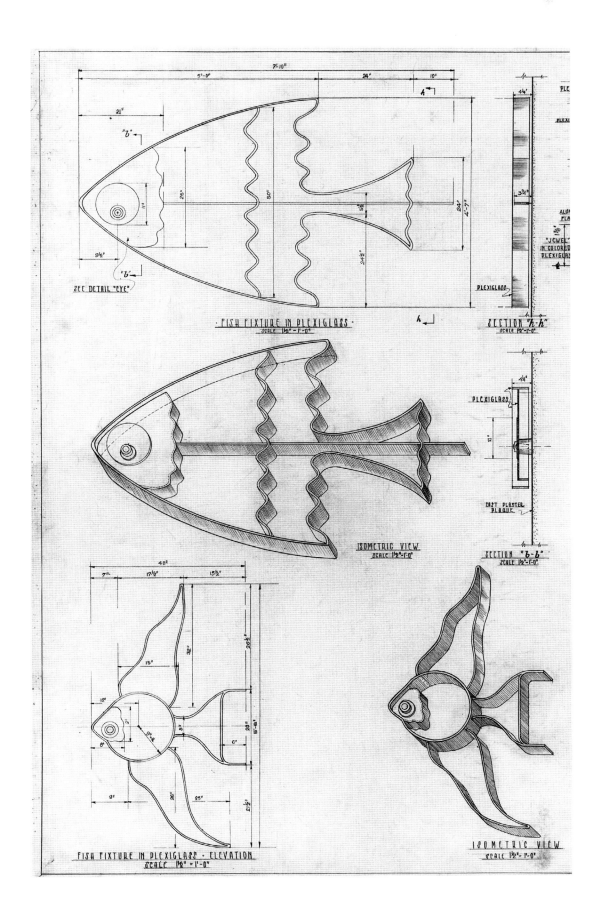

SEE DETAIL "EYE"

FISH FIXTURE IN PLEXIGLASS
SCALE 1½" = 1'-0"

SECTION "h-h"
SCALE 1½"=1'-0"

ISOMETRIC VIEW
SCALE 1½"=1'-0"

PLEXIGLASS

CAST PLASTER
PLAQUE

SECTION "b-b"
SCALE 1½"=1'-0"

FISH FIXTURE IN PLEXIGLASS - ELEVATION
SCALE 1½" = 1'-0"

ISOMETRIC VIEW
SCALE 1½" = 1'-0"

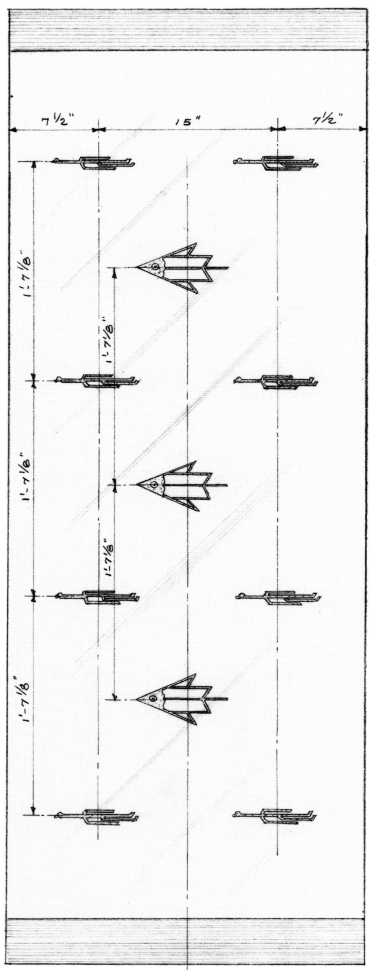

7 ½"   1 5 "   7 ½"

1'-7⅛"

1'-7⅛"

1'-7⅛"

1'-7⅛"

1'-7⅛"

Stylized fish designs graced the front door and embraced the stage. Large cartouches made of Plexiglas and ornamental plaster framed the proscenium arch. They seemed like floating sheets with their mystic designs of undersea life illuminated with the latest in hidden lighting effects. The predominant color was sea green.

One entered the interior of the theater into a patio-foyer that measured forty feet from stone floor to ceiling. This inner lobby was open to the sky, and the sun shined in. Free-form mirrors on one wall reflected the colored oolite stone and waterfalls of the opposing wall.

The Carib auditorium seated two thousand and seventy-seven people on its main floor and balcony. It offered the latest and the best in comfort and technology. The main floor seats were Kroehler 'push-backs," high in the back and fully constructed with latex rubber. The upstairs smoking section used Heywood-Wakefield chairs, a newly developed rocking chair for theaters. A broad concrete staircase, considered an unusual engineering achievement and one of the early efforts at "floating stairs," led to the mezzanine. An escalator could take you there as well.

The contour curtain of the Carib was of tangerine hammered satin with borders of emerald green satin. An additional pair of curtains were deep bottle green plush. The screen curtain itself was translucent turquoise rayon ripple repp, decorated with a hand-dyed mural of marine life found in the Caribbean waters. Two baroque octopi behaved like sentries guarding the stage. The octopi were indirectly lit, causing the proscenium arch to appear to float in mid-air.

More than forty firms were contracted to participate in the construction and embellishment of the Carib Theatre. Thirty-five were located in the greater Miami area, making this a "Made in Miami" showcase.

Live macaws and other multi-colored birds dwelled in this tropical palace for many years, bringing to life the entire panorama.

Design and details for the front door of the Carib Theater from the architectural plans, 1950.

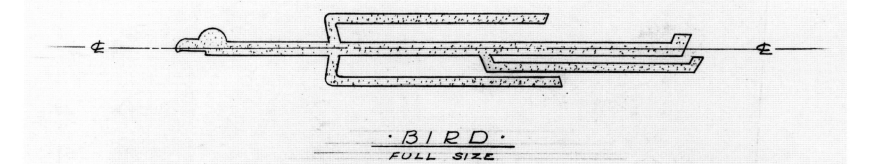

· BIRD ·
FULL SIZE

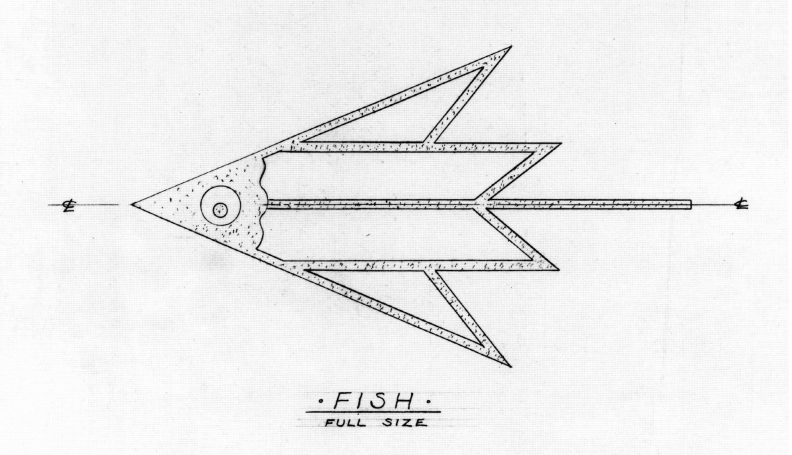

· FISH ·
FULL SIZE

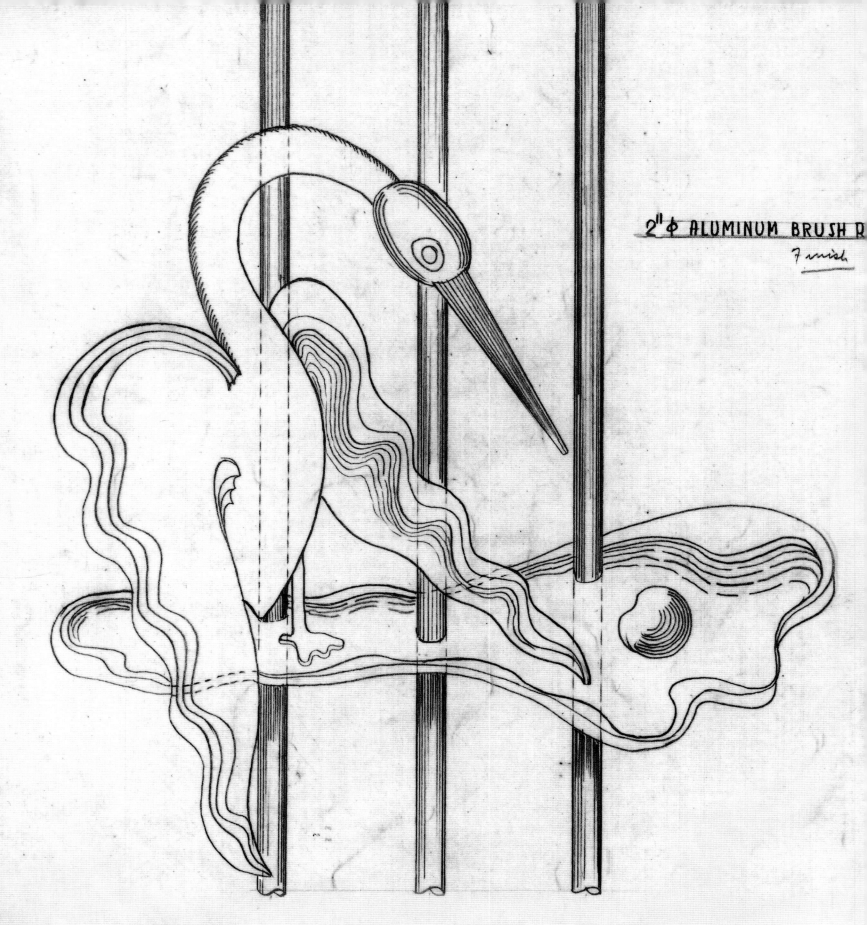

2" Φ ALUMINUM BRUSH R

Finish

"BIRDS" PLEXIGLAS FIXTURES ON ALUMINUM RODS

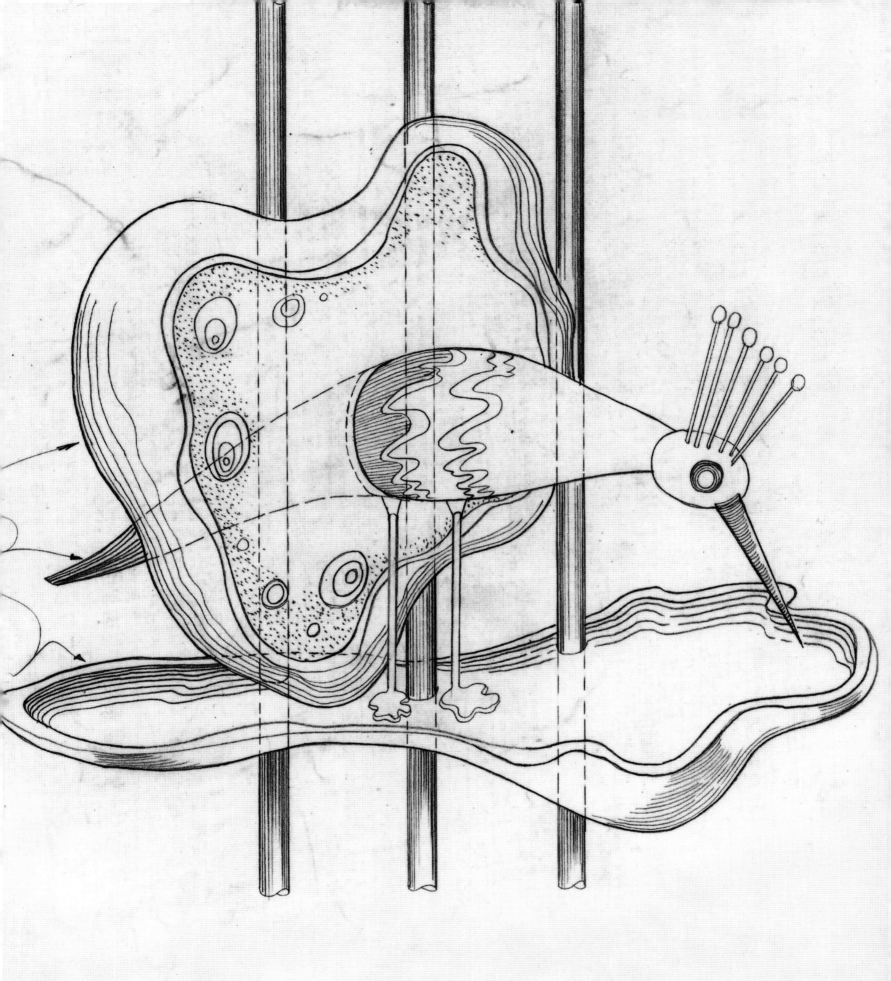

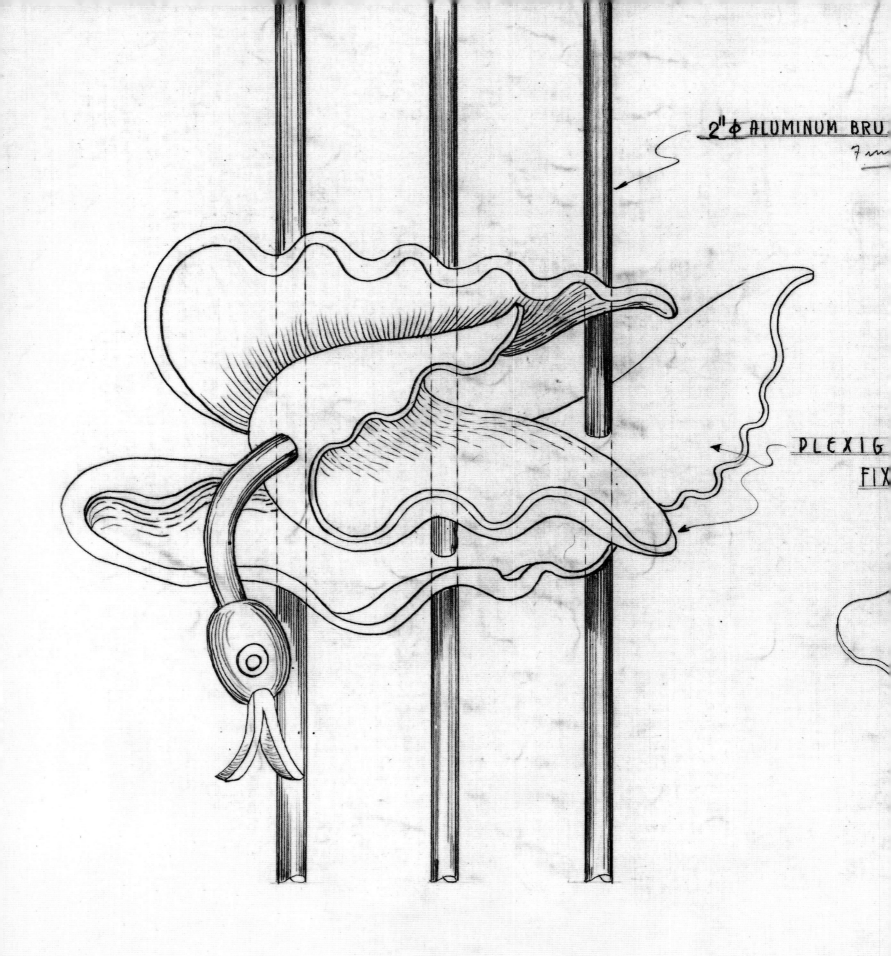

2" Φ ALUMINUM BRU
7 m

PLEXIG
FIX

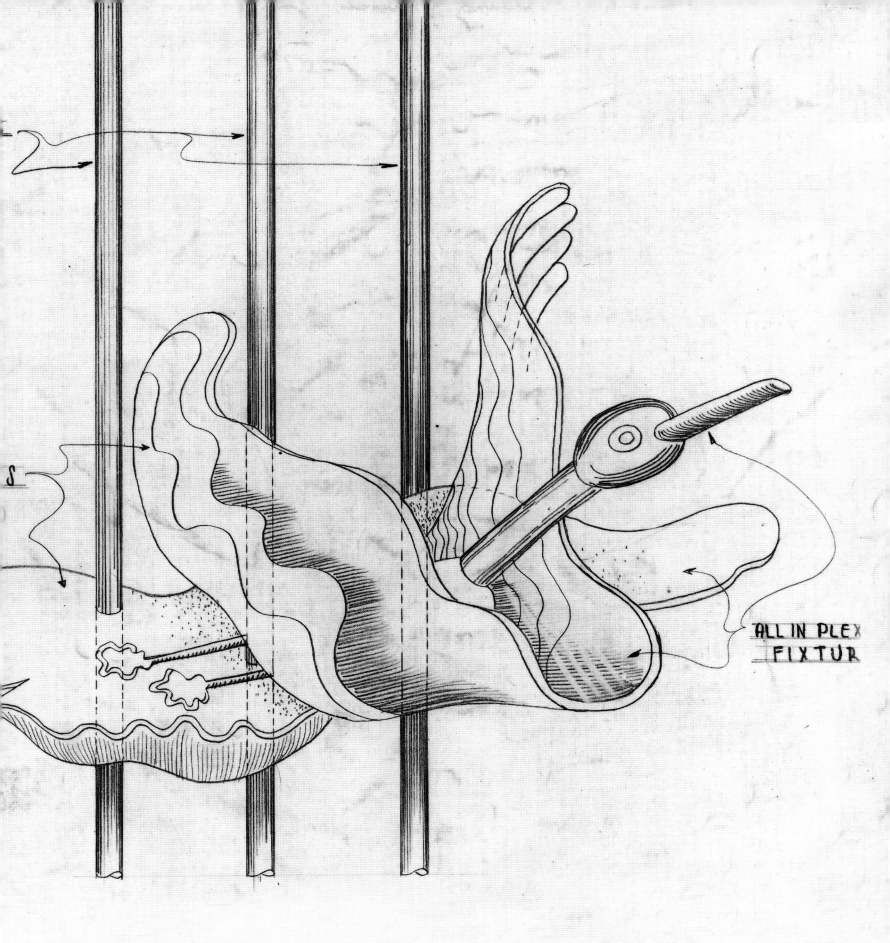

ALL IN PLEX
FIXTUR

235

Opposite:
Detail of winning drawing submission for the Carib Theatre competition, Miami Beach, c. late 1940s. Michael J. DeAngelis, Architect.

Below:
Inaugural program for opening night The proceeds were given to the Damon Runyon Cancer Fund, Variety Children's Hospital, Mt. Sinai Hospital, and St. Francis Hospital. Twentieth Century-Fox donated *The Mudlark* for this purpose.

THE
Carib

SOUVENIR PROGRAMME
INAUGURAL PERFORMANCE
FRIDAY, DECEMBER 22, 1950

Carib Capsule

With an assist from usher Richard Ramberg, Sidney Meyer and Mitchell Wolfson lower the heavy "Carib Capsule" into its underground vault to remain for twenty-five years. The burial was part of the ground-breaking ceremonies on Friday afternoon for the new Carib theater on Lincoln Road in Miami Beach. The Carib was the thirtieth theater in the Wometco chain, owned and operated by Wolfson and Meyer. Forty-three years later, during the renovation of Lincoln Road in 1996, construction workers installing drainage pipes uncovered the capsule. The capsule contained, among many other items, a strand of pearls worn by June Allyson in the film *The Glenn Miller Story* and a sheath of letters from celebrities including Laurence Olivier.

Opposite:
Prop Key

Mayor Kenneth Oka examining prop key to the City of Miami Beach before handing it to Janet Leigh, who is best remembered for the forty-five minutes that she was on the screen in Alfred Hitchcock's thriller *Psycho*. Real keys were actually given to the celebrities as keepsakes. These were life-sized, bronze, and inscribed with the words, "World's Playground." They were reserved for more private moments of exchange. Miss Leigh's dress, tropical goddess style, brings to life the tropical backdrop of the Carib Theatre curtain.

Hollywood at the Carib

At the time these photographs were taken, Wometco was bringing Hollywood to Miami Beach. There were four first-run movie houses on Lincoln Road alone: the Beach, the Lincoln, the Colony, and the Carib.

Geraldine Page in a limousine following the 1962 world premiere of the film version of Tennessee Williams' *Sweet Bird of Youth*. Miss Page received rave reviews for her performance. Note the prop keys to the city in the background.

At the stage door of the Carib Theatre, from left to right: Kenneth Oka, Mitchell Wolfson, Robert Evans, Jill St. John and Sidney Meyer

The Kid Stays in the Picture
A young Robert Evans right before he became Paramount's "boy king." Evans's life story reads like a Hollywood film. Son of a Manhattan dentist, he was a child radio star discovered by the legendary Darryl F. Zanuck. Evans spent

He made Ali McGraw a major star in *Love Story* and then married her. In a much publicized defection, Ali McGraw left Robert Evans for Steve McQueen.

In 2003, Evans released a celebratory narrative of his life, "The Kid Stays in the Picture," composed of newsreel footage, stills, and haunting shots of his mansion in various states of glory and disrepair. Evans himself narrates in a gravelly voice: his speech

The Stars at Night
Hollywood on Miami's Stage Set

"'To the first time visitor
its (Miami's) shining spires,
its tropical foliage,
the incredible blue of its water,
the cloud formations
that tower in the background—
all sharply etched under
an intense, white sunlight—
appear as a motion-picture set.'
And at night,
the Stars came out."

Federal Writers' Project

Previous spread:
**Florida skyline state
tree, Sabal palms**

Left:
In 1939, when the
unemployed writers of
the **Federal Writers'
Project** described
Miami for the *Florida
Guide*, they didn't
revisit the boom of the
1920s. Instead, they
foreshadowed the
fifties.[1]

MITCHELL WOLFSON JUNIOR
5030 NORTH BAY ROAD · MIAMI BEACH, FLORIDA 33140

Dear Michele,

And at night, the stars come out lighting
up the beach with a dazzle competing with the
moon itself. The whole scene appeared like
a motion picture set for some Hollywood
melodrama determinedly located in the realm of
fantasy. Miami Beach attracted them like horse
flies to native honey. I remember all those
spectacular movie premieres and fancy night
clubs populated with the extravagant and the
excessive of once-upon-a-time.

Micky

Playful Chico Marx
Kenneth Oka with
Chico Marx at The
Rhythm Club, Wofford
Hotel, Miami Beach,
possibly 1946.

**"I was President of
the Miami Beach
Junior Chamber of
Commerce and
invited Chico Marx
to speak. The
Jaycees were
always promoting
the local economy
and extolling the
local scene. We
used to meet at
the old Wofford
Hotel [Olive
Wofford was one
of the pioneers
of Miami Beach].
Marx spoke
movingly and
sincerely."**
From Kenneth Oka's
recollections

**"People ask me
where I like it
better, California
or Florida. . .
I've spent a lot
of time in both,
and I've learned
that home
is where your
friends are."**
Chico Marx

Eternal Starlet
Terry Moore arrives in Miami on Eastern Air Lines for the premier of *The Return of October*, December 5, 1948. Her full length mink coat was more of a prop than a necessity for the mild Florida winter. Moore began her screen career at age eleven and developed into a busty Hollywood sexpot. Though she was nominated for an Oscar in the supporting category for *Come Back, Little Sheba* in 1953, Moore generally received more press for her romantic escapades. Her much publicized dates included Henry Kissinger and Howard Hughes, whom she reportedly married in secret.[2]

"A bright new celestial body in filmdom's firmament"
Wometco press release

Opposite:
Unknown Starlet
With Howard Hughes peering over her right shoulder and Frank Sinatra striding behind her unidentified escort, this starlet is in good company. Sonny Shepherd, Wometco executive and creator of the original "Mickey Mouse Club," is on the far right.

Sinatra wintered at the Fontainebleau Hotel in the 1950s and 60s. Floyd McSwaine remembered them all: Dean Martin, Sammy Davis Jr., Joey Bishop, and Sinatra.
"When he walked in the lobby, people would stand up and say, 'Hey, Frank.' They were crazy about him. He could have been President of the United States."[3]

A Song in My Heart
Jane Froman and Captain Burn, her husband, with Burnett Bernie Roth, Vice-Mayor of Miami Beach, and Mitchell Wolfson in front of the Carib Theatre for the opening of *With a Song In My Heart*, the biography of Froman and her husband, who was a Pan American pilot. 1952

Another world premiere for Wometco, the film featured actress Susan Hayward as singer Jane Froman, making her comeback after an air crash left her almost completely crippled. Froman actually did most of the singing with Hayward miming. The film won an Oscar for Best Score.

Mad Wednesday
Harold Lloyd, Arline Judge, Sonny Shepherd, and Sidney Meyer at the premier of *Mad Wednesday*.[4]

Arline Judge started her career as a Broadway chorus dancer in her teens, and later was a member of Jimmy Durante's nightclub act. Although she was largely forgettable as an actress, she became known through her many marriages: her seven husbands included director Wesley Ruggles and former Brooklyn Dodgers owner Daniel Topping.

Harold Lloyd is best remembered today as the young man dangling desperately from a clock tower in the 1923 classic *Safety Last*. At the height of his career, Lloyd was one of the most popular and highest-paid stars of his time.

Show-Woman
Ava Gardner on preview morning of the premiere in Washington, D.C. of *The Snows of Kilimanjaro*, September 14, 1952. Mitchell Wolfson, on the right, retiring President of the Theatre Owners of America, with his fellow showmen and conventioneers.

Show-woman as well as actress, Ava Gardner personally met the operators of 4,900 leading motion picture theaters in the United States. When *The Snows of Kilimanjaro* opened in Miami, the famed U.S. Marine Corps Band serenaded her outside of The Miami theatre.

The Snows of Kilimanjaro
Based on Ernest Hemingway's rambling novel about a writer seeking purpose and meaning, *The Snows of Kilimanjaro* had a powerhouse line-up of stars. The critics, however, considered it to be somewhat of a disappointment.

Never Lost a Fight

Judge Kenneth Oka and Gertrude Oka with **Rocky Marciano** at the 1955 opening of *Rocky's*, a short-lived Miami restaurant. Known as "The Brockton Block-buster," Rocco Francis Marchegiano never lost a professional fight. Beginning in 1947, Rocky fought forty-nine times and won every bout, forty-three by knockouts. He beat Joe Louis in the eighth round of their match in 1951, and ko'ed Jersey Joe Walcott in the thirteenth to take the Heavyweight Title in 1952. He defended the crown six times and retired from boxing undefeated.

"I'd get low, making myself a smaller target, a tougher man to hit on the chin. My game was always to bob and weave and never let myself be maneuvered out in the middle of the ring."
Rocky on himself [5]

"Great heavyweights, like [Joe] Louis, had the loneliness of the ages in their silence, and men like Marciano were mystified by a power which seemed to have been granted them."
Norman Mailer on Rocky [6]

Note Gertrude's silver belt buckle, an official souvenir from London, commemorating the coronation of Queen Elizabeth II in 1953.

Saint Joan at the Carib Theatre
Kenneth Oka presents a prop Key to the City of Miami Beach to **Jean Seberg** at the Carib Theatre, February 1957. Seberg was appearing in her first film, Otto Preminger's *Saint Joan*. The movie was a disaster, but Seberg became a star.

"She was very young. So was I."
Kenneth Oka

A few years after *Saint Joan*, Seberg, who was from Marshaltown, Iowa, became a European icon in Jean-Luc Godard's *Breathless*. Her image—casually seductive with boyish hair—stuck, but her career, marriages, and love affairs floundered. She became involved with the Black Panthers, which led the FBI to spy on her and plot a smear campaign. Seberg committed suicide at the age of forty.

Carlos Fuentes wrote a wonderful short novel, *Diana*, a roman à clef about the author's affair with Jean Seberg. Published in 1995, it is set in 1970, when Seberg's movie fame was behind her.

"I watched my lover sacrifice and discipline herself for a profession in which she didn't believe, in which she could not see herself, in which she could not even glimpse the future."
Diana, Carlos Fuentes

**"Anita Ekberg had
skin like alabaster.
She was wearing
no bra. She was a
big girl."**
Kenneth Oka

Champagne

The design of champagne glasses has undergone a mild
revolution. Originally, the bubbly beverage was sipped from
a stemmed saucer shaped glass reputedly modeled after
the round breast of Queen Marie Antoinette. As wine
drinking has become a more serious occupation, long,
fluted glasses that better contain the sparkling bubbles of
the champagne have been recommended.

Belting It Out
Polly Bergen belts it out with live orchestra accompaniment on the Fontainebleau stage, early 1960s. Note the bar glass motif on her sequined dress: a cocktail mix of sparkle and dazzle.

Bergen is best known for her Emmy-award winning performance in the 1957 movie, *The Helen Morgan Story*. She recorded Morgan's signature song, "Why Was I Born," and is still singing it today.

The former Nelli Paulina Burgin of Bluegrass, Tennessee, started out as a hillbilly singer on radio and with big bands, but she had only one goal in mind when she arrived in New York at the age of nineteen.

"'I was *fanatically* ambitious,' she said. 'All I ever wanted was to be a star. I didn't want to be a singer. I didn't want to be an actress. I wanted to be a *star*.'"

WESTERN UNION
TELEGRAM

CLASS OF SERVICE
This is a fast message unless its deferred character is indicated by the proper symbol.

SYMBOLS
DL=Day Letter
NL=Night Letter
LT=International Letter Telegram

W. P. MARSHALL, PRESIDENT

The filing time shown in the date line on domestic telegrams is STANDARD TIME at point of origin. Time of receipt is STANDARD TIME at point of destination

1201

AA68 SSE60

1958 JAN 2 PM 1 51

A MZY005 PD=MIAMI FLO 2 NFT=
:MAYOR AND MRS KENNETH OKLA=
2801 FAIRGREEN DR MIAMI BEACH FLO=

:WOULD BE DELIGHTED IF YOU WOULD JOIN US AT A COCKTAIL
PARTY FRIDAY SEVEN TO NINE PM PAVILLION ROOM EDEN ROC
HOTEL HOPE YOU WILL ATTEND WILL BE LOOKING FORWARD TO
MEETING YOU SINCERELY=
POLLY BERGEN RSVP RONNIE MCNICHOLAS PLAZA 8-8731=

THE COMPANY WILL APPRECIATE SUGGESTIONS FROM ITS PATRONS CONCERNING ITS SERVICE

Cinema Goddess at the Stage Door
Janet Leigh, in a tight tropical dress, hangs on Mayor Kenneth Oka's arm. The event was the opening of *The Perfect Furlough* starring Miss Leigh and Tony Curtis, 1958.

Opposite:
The Best of Everything
Sammy Walsh, Robert Evans, Jill St. John and Mayor Kenneth Oka at the Carib Theatre stage door. This could have been the premiere of *The Best of Everything*, 1959, a trashy, very enjoyable soap opera in which Robert Evans played a small part. Young Evans, not yet the "Kid Mogul," was spending a lot of time between Havana and Miami.

Jill St. John is the personification of Hollywood glamour in her black lace gown. She was a vivacious leading lady throughout the 60s and 70s. Among other roles, she starred as the James Bond beauty, Tiffany Case, in Diamonds are Forever in 1971. Well-built and red-headed, she was typically cast as an empty-headed broad, but in reality was known to be quite intelligent. She married actor Robert Wagner in 1990, on her fourth trip down the aisle.[9]

In later years, after decades on the Miami nightclub circuit, Sammy Walsh became host at Herb and Al Login's Place for Steak on the 79th Street Causeway.

"Wometco at this time was bringing down lots of premier movies, first run shows, opening in Miami Beach. They brought the stars down here. At that time there were four movie houses on Lincoln Road alone: The Beach, the Lincoln, the Colony, and the Carib."
Kenneth Oka

Top Producer
Mitchell Wolfson with **Richard and Lili Zanuck** at a press cocktail party in their honor at the Eden Roc Hotel, Friday, March 13, 1959. In the early fifties, the star-packed Zanuck production, *The Snows of Kilimanjaro,* was featured at Wometco's Town Theatre in Miami.

After starting in the motion picture business as production assistant for his father, the legendary Darryl F. Zanuck, Richard went on to have an illustrious career and become a distinguished leader in the motion picture industry. When he was awarded the Irving G. Thalberg Memorial Award in 1991, he became its only second-generation recipient.

Richard Zanuck's blockbuster hits include *The Sting, Jaws,* and *Driving Miss Daisy,* winner of four Academy Awards, including Best Picture. Lili Zanuck made her directorial debut with the critically acclaimed *Rush* in 1992, having shared production credits with her husband on *Driving Miss Daisy* and many other films.[10]

"You've got to gamble. The movie industry isn't a slide-rule business and never will be. It's the world's biggest crap game."[11]
Richard Zanuck's mantra

SHIRLEY MacLAINE
1967 STAR OF YEAR

PAUL NEWMAN
1967 STAR OF YEAR

A bemused Paul
Newman and a serene
Shirley MacLaine
on the dais with
Mitchell Wolfson at
the National Association
of Theatre Owners
banquet at Morris
Lapidus's Americana
Hotel, Miami Beach,
October 24, 1967.

Top Stars
Shirley MacLaine was
named "Top Female
Star of the Year" and
accepted a silver tray at
the podium. The
lengthy encomium
etched on the tray took
so long to read that
the next day's *Herald*
reported that whoever
wrote it must have
gotten space rates.
Paul Newman was
named "Top Male Star
of the Year."

Hy Gardner reported
in the *Herald* that
toastmaster Mitchell
Wolfson performed
brilliantly, dissolving the
barrier between the
diners anc the dais.

The Duke

John Wayne was one of the most popular box-office stars of all time. For an incredible twenty-five years, he was rated at the top in box-office appeal. Born Marion Michael Morrison in Winterset, Iowa, he picked up the nickname Duke from his Airedale of that name. An innovator in the film industry, Duke tossed aside the model of the good guy cowboy and created a tougher, deeper-dimensioned Western hero.

Mitchell Wolfson with John Wayne and his elegant wife Pilar, who sports a bouffant hair style. An ardent fan in splendid regalia is obviously dazzled by the presence of stardom.

"He gave the whole world the image of what an American should be."
Elizabeth Taylor, testifying in favor of the Congressional Gold Medal struck for John Wayne, 1978

269

World's Playground
Keys to the City

Michele,

Of all the major twentieth-century American cities, only Miami lacks a logical past. It had no historic foundation to unearth, build on, or celebrate. It rose from its mire at the time of the great empire builders, Flagler and land developers, Fisher. If Miami Beach was built on anything at all it was the bedrock of illusion. Admittedly this was, at least in the beginning, a major embarrassment to you and me in a world which we had become familiar with that derived civic dignity and culture from the European model. So now we have set out to show how Miami Beach came to be part of the traditional construct. Does this mean that we too have become propagandists for a borrowed past? But in constructing a spurious biography, it must be said that Miami Beach never settled for mere imitation or replication. The city always had a sense of its own distinctiveness that allowed it to adapt any and all reference to it in order to further promote its peculiar identity. This persistent recycling of appropriation in a context of boasted originality led to continual self-reinvention for the city as long as the protagonist discharged their hyperbole. No city was ever more clever at escaping the anxiety of bad press. And weren't our fathers old pros? They were, and I guess we are, able to do what we do because of a readiness to remember the new as well as the old. Our pragmatic natures as stubborn as our creative ones, have lead us to adapt not only what we inherited but also what we could imagine, showing a confidence in our own identity even in the face of unprecedented change.

Micky

RALLY

TUESDAY EVENING MAY 14, 1957

8 P. M.

LABOR LYCEUM

25 WASHINGTON AVENUE

ENTERTAINMENT
REFRESHMENTS
AND

JUDGE
KENNETH
OKA

Candidate for City Council

Bring Your Friends — All Welcome

Campaign announcement for Judge Kenneth Oka, candidate for City Council, inviting the Yiddish speaking voters in Miami Beach to go to the polls and elect him Councilman. The turnout was effective, and Oka received the highest number of votes, becoming Mayor.

A widely regarded and
eccentric humorist,
Damon Runyan was
one of the most
popular writers in
America the first half of
the twentieth century.
Runyan's stories of the
underworld had wide
appeal, and *Guys and
Dolls*, a romanticized
fiction written in 1931,
had the most success.
Adapted to music,
Guys and Dolls opened
on Broadway in 1951
and ran for twelve
hundred performances.
The movie, starring
Marlon Brando and
Frank Sinatra, was also
a hit.

The word "runyanesque"
has entered the lexicon,
indicating a good-
hearted urbanite from
a lower social order.
When he wrote the
piece on Mitchell
Wolfson for the Miami
Herald, Damon Runyan
stuck close to his
formula—tender and
palatable fare. When
Runyan died in 1946,
World War I flying ace
Eddie Rickenbacker
flew over Broadway and
scattered his ashes.

Right:
Miami *Herald*,
May 20, 1941

TUESDAY, MAY 20, 1941

Damon Runyon

Mitch Wolfson Is Queer Guy Who Really Likes To Help His Town

MITCHELL WOLFSON, a citizen of Miami Beach, down here in Dade county, Florida, is deemed somewhat eccentric by many of his friends because, though reputed a millionaire, he is running for re-election as an $1,800 a year councilman of his home town.

It cost him $8,000 to win by one or two votes two years ago, his first political venture, and then he had a three months battle in court about it. He has reduced his campaign overhead by $6,000 this time, but still his friends cannot see why he is bidding for the headaches of municipal office when he might be devoting himself with more pleasure and certainly with more profit to the 20 or more movie houses he owns and controls with his brother-in-law, Sidney Meyer, in the Greater Miami area.

Wolfson, 41, good looking, and affable, may be explained, however, by a story that is told of how he first got mixed up in politics without even having had any previous experience in that curious game. It is said that shortly before the election two years ago some of his fellow citizens were expressing concern about the future government of Miami Beach as foreshadowed by the political trend and deploring the lack of what they deemed high grade candidate material for the council.

Wolfson shared in this concern and said he would do anything he could to improve the situation, and what about some of the deplorers stepping in and running? But it seems they were like the most of us, excellent critics, but reluctant to take any active part in proceedings, an attitude that pained and surprised him no little.

"Hah!" he said. "You all complain, but none of you are willing to stick your necks out. I'll run myself."

HIS campaign is still vividly remembered in Miami Beach as a sort of continuous movie preview, for Wolfson's first step after filing his petition in candidacy was to summon the publicity staff and the best showmen of his movie chain and instruct them to get busy selling him to the public as a candidate. The resultant blast of electric signs, photographic blow-ups, newspaper publicity, flags, bands, radio stuff, entertainments and even refreshments, startled the community. Some of the folks got the idea that Clark Gable was running for office in a new picture.

Wolfson campaigned as a business man interested in the conduct of the city's business. We are told that he has made a good councilman, too, displaying great conscientiousness on his job, and putting over a number of ideas that were to the benefit of Miami Beach. Once in politics, he got in plumb up to his neck and during the last gubernatorial campaign he handled the Miami Beach campaign for Spessard L. Holland, the winner.

WOLFSON was born in Key West and went to grammar school there, but completed his education at Erasmus Hall in Brooklyn and Columbia. His father and mother came to the United States from Botka, Russia, in 1887 and soon settled in Key West, where the father, Louis Wolfson, opened a dry goods business. He refused to wait on customers who could not speak English and, as Key West had a big population of Cubans at that time, this idiosyncrasy probably cost Louis Wolfson a lot of business, but it is also said to have made a lot of the population study English because they liked his store.

Wearing a handsome
double breasted white
linen suit with mother of
pearl buttons and a
white gardenia in his
lapel, an ebullient
Mitchell Wolfson stands
behind the Mayor's
desk in City Hall after
being elected Mayor of
Miami Beach. His world
is framed by baskets
containing roses and
gladiolus from well
wishers.

Mitchell Wolfson had
specific ideas regarding
government when he
was elected Mayor of
Miami Beach on June
2, 1941. The ideas
were a legacy from his
father, Louis, who used
to tell him,

**"Mitchell, you can't
grow a crop
every year unless
you put something
back into the
soil."**

Louis Wolfson thought
that everyone should
devote part of his life in
service to one's fellow
man, and that every
human being has
spiritual importance.
Both Wolfsons
often articulated the
philosophy,

**"What helps one
helps all, what
hurts one, hurts
all."**

Courting the Media
At the Stork Club in the famous Cub Room, the new Mayor of Miami Beach is interviewed by New York newspaper men. Left to right: Edward Kennelly, New York *Post*; Harry Factor, New York *Sun*; James Kenny, New York *World Telegram*; Bill Dresser, New York *Sun*; Don Short, New York *Journal American*; Mayor Wolfson; Dick Dunlap and Jimmy Sykes, New York *Herald Tribune*; John Irving, New York *Journal American*; Joe Gessick, New York *Post*; Joe Copps, Steve Hannagan office (a public relations firm). c. 1941

"**Mayor Mitchell Wolfson, newly-elected head man of Miami Beach, tells New York newspaper men that Miami Beach is working on a ten-year plan to provide municipal facilities to care for 150,000 home owners and visitors after the war as he is interviewed at a luncheon in the Cub Room of the famous Stork Club.**"
Press release, Steve Hannagan, 1943

The Birth of Café Society

The Stork Club, at 3 East 53rd Street (now Paley Park) was founded as a front for jazz age mobsters by Oklahoma bootlegger Sherman Billingsley. From the speak-easy era to the Vietnam War, it was the nation's most storied night spot, a posh oasis for starlets and millionaires. According to Billingsley, Ernest Hemingway tried to pay a bar bill one night with a $100,000 movie royalty check. Mr. Billingsley made the change. Another evening, Hemingway got into a shoving match with Lewis E. Laws, the warden of Sing Sing, and knocked him down. Billingsley felt that:

"One fight a year is good publicity provided the fighters are big names."

Some of the items considered standard at the lunch table fifty years ago are no longer common: ashtrays, centerpieces of carnations and fuzzy ferns, and iced relish containers with celery sticks and olives. Matches, hard to find today, were the ultimate status symbol, taken home and displayed. The Stork Club ended its reign with a bitter strike, and Mr. Billingsley's death in 1966.

Swimming in the Winter

While Miami Beach chilled to air temperatures of fifty-one degrees, Mayor Kenneth Oka participated in a publicity stunt for tourism. A swim in the ocean was staged to lure northerners to sunny Florida. The country was experiencing a particularly harsh winter.

Photos from Oka's demonstration of tropical faith were published in newspapers nationwide, including the December 15, 1962 issues of the Newark *Evening News*, Chicago *Sun-Times*, and Rochester *Democrat and Chronicle,* as well as the December 16, 1962 issue of the Atlanta *Journal and Constitution*.

This direct marketing ploy took place at Lummus Park, the celebrated stretch of beach now the infamous South Beach, a perennial favorite for surf bathing and display. In the background, the Tides Hotel under scaffolding, a Deco masterpiece by architect L. Murray Dixon.

Dishing Dirt with the Ladies

Silhouetted by an animated Australian pine, the ladies of the Miami Beach Garden Club break ground ceremoniously. The garden center was to include rare tropical plants, a classroom with a qualified horticulturalist and, most importantly, to provide a focus for the gardening ladies and their groups. The local Garden Clubs were all represented: Miami Beach, Tropical, Mt. Sinai, and Islands. A library and gardening information service was envisioned as well. The Miami Beach Garden Club was responsible for millions of flowers planted on the city's 828 acres of streets, parkways, golf courses and parks. Note the Girl Scouts in attendance.

Shovels never had a more glamorous role than at the ground breaking ceremony. They were daintily decorated with flowers and ribbons. The ladies, too, were decked out in flowers, and many used white gloves for the occasion. On the far right, Mrs. Herbert Frick, Chairman of the Committee that made it all possible, shovels dirt with a gold-plated spade. Mayor Kenneth Oka, on the far left, helps break ground.

Miami Beach was famous for its landscaping program. City Managers from forty-six states who attended a conference at the nearby Convention Center were awed by the organization and output of the Miami Beach Parks Department. Its assembly-line pattern of flower production, hidden from view behind the Convention Hall at Washington Avenue and 17th Street, was unrivaled by any other city. The visiting City Managers took home scaled down blueprints for their own nurseries and souvenir roses.

Previous spread:
**Greeting
Miss Universe**
Marlene Schmitt,
a radiant Miss Universe
beaming gamma rays,
with Mayor Oka on
her left in a summer
tuxedo, flanked by Mr.
and Mrs. David Schine.

**". . .for five years
I've been trying
unsuccessfully to
catch up with my
reputation of
devoting all of my
official time to
tape-measuring
beauty contestants"**
Mayor Kenneth Oka
to the New York *World
Telegram and Sun*, in
an article titled "Sunny
Days in Miami Beach"

The Miss Universe
Pageant moved from
Long Beach, California
to Miami Beach in
1960. Broadcast to a
world audience, the
contest generated
tremendous publicity.
The sparkle and
glamour of the spectacle
dove-tailed perfectly
with the city's image.
The pageant was
dubbed the most
profitable promotion in
the United States.

Hillevi Schine, ever
glamorous, is a former
Swedish National
Decathlon champion,
Miss Sweden, and
Miss Universe, 1955.
Here she wears a white
lace gown overlaying
satin with a satin strap
emphasizing her waist.

The new Miss
Universe, formerly Miss
Germany, wears a
strapless Shantung silk
ball gown with a
beaded bodice and
long satin gloves. She
carries the emblematic
scepter. On her head
is a jeweled crown with
its all-encompassing
symbol of fanciful
whirling electrons,
the logo of post-war
euphoria. The launching
of Sputnik three years
earlier and the iconic
335-foot-high Atomium
of the 1958 World's Fair
in Brussels, Belgium,
cast a long shadow.
Vast stores of energy
promised release
as well as a new world
order.

David Schine was the
very handsome scion
of the J. Myer Schine
family. Their hotel
empire spanned both
coasts, and today is
consolidated in the
Beverly Wilshire Hotel.
The Schine family
bought Miami Beach's
treasure, The Roney
Plaza, in 1943 and sold
it in 1966. In his
mid-twenties, David
Schine gained great
exposure as the chief
consultant to Senator
Joe McCarthy's
Permanent Subcomittee
on Investigations in the
Senate. During the
investigation into
communist activities in
the spring of 1953,
McCarthy fought
a tough battle against
real and imagined
communist infiltration of
the government. The
hearings resulted in the
blacklisting of many fine
Americans who were
accused of being too
far to the left for the
comfort of the right,
and proved to be not
only a defining moment
for post-war America,
but also an illustration
of the power of
television to shape
opinion. Amidst rumor
and innuendo, Schine
left Washington and
devoted himself to the
hotel business. He
married the former Miss
Sweden, and began a
family. In later years,
David Schine tried his
hand at film making,
achieving success in
1971 as the executive
producer of the Oscar-
winning thriller, *The
French Connection*. He
died in a plane crash
in 1996.

Hostesses for Beauty

A luncheon in honor of the new Miss Universe, Germany's Marlene Schmidt, was held in the Boom Boom Room at the Fontainebleau Hotel. Members of the Miss Universe Beauty Pageant Hostesses and Chaperones Executive Committee were responsible for guiding and advising the beauty contestants when they competed for the scepter and the crown. Many of the hostesses were multilingual and helped make the stay of foreign beauty queens more comfortable. The hostesses were present for all pageant functions and remained with the girls day and night, caring for them as if they were their own daughters. Some of the hostesses include Gertrude Oka, seated on the left. Next to Gertrude, also seated, is long-time hostess and organizer Inez Krensky, with Marlene Schmitt, Miss Universe, seated to her left. On the table is an edible centerpiece, a cruise ship, in miniature, from the port of Miami. Standing between Inez Krensky and Miss Universe is Helen Lipp, wife of the Miami Beach City Manager. Also pictured are Mrs. Seymour H. Fine and Therese Beckman.

Ambassador to South America

Like the Carib Theatre Goddess come to life, Miss Andrea Vasconcellos de Oliveiria from Londrina, Brazil, coffee capital of the world, presents a golden sieve to Mayor Kenneth Oka at City Hall, Miami Beach, 1961. The sieve is filled with coffee beans, and the Mayor is smiling at the presentation and the intoxicating aroma. Miss Vasconcellos de Oliveiria is fantastically outfitted in a one-shouldered dress made of the burlap traditionally used to package coffee beans. The burlap is fringed to create a three-tiered skirt which in turn is hemmed by a garland of blossoms and leaves. A corsage of coffee blossoms graces her left shoulder. Her earrings, bracelet, and belt are all composed of coffee beans. On Andrea Vasconcellos de Oliveiria, every aspect of the product and its packaging have been used to maximum effect.

The event was part of a nineteen-day official tour sponsored by Varig Airlines and headquartered at the Fontainebleau Hotel. The Brazilian guests were feted by Fontainebleau President Ben Novak. After declaring Miami "clean, friendly, and fabulous" in *Entre Nous*, the printed voice of the hotel, the Brazilians departed by car caravan for other cities in the United States.

Fiddling while Miami Builds

Mayor of Miami Beach, Kenneth Oka, shares a musical interlude on top of a construction site with the Mayor of Miami, Robert King High. Noted syndicated columnist Hy Gardener wears a microphone to broadcast this marketing stunt. Oka previously played violin in the University of Miami's eighth season, 1935 to 1936. He continued playing in the string section of the Miami Beach Symphonette during the 1950s. Robert King High was a popular four-term Mayor from 1957 to 1967 and a long-time advocate of low cost housing for the area's senior and less affluent citizens. Mayor High had aspirations to be in a political arena larger than Dade County, and this event was most likely a part of one of his unsuccessful campaigns for Florida Governor. Robert King High died quite young of a sudden heart attack.

Coffee plants are evergreen, and flower in a continuous cycle. The flowers emit a strong, pleasant perfume. The leaves are deep green, glossy and fleshy, not unlike laurel leaves with a characteristic wavy edge. The coffee crop grows in zones with no seasonal climatic changes, a world that exists somewhere between spring and summer. Brazil, the world's leading coffee producer, fills twenty to thirty million burlap bags each year.

Receiving Foreign Dignitaries

Mayor Kenneth Oka greets visiting dignitaries from Chad including Mr. Adoum Ahmet, Mr. Abdoulaye Lamana, and Mr. Silas Selingar. Guests of the Department of State under the Foreign Leader Program, these visiting dignitaries from Chad provide a vision of time and space. To the left, wearing the elegant robes of his ancestors, is Mr. Adoum Ahmet. At the time of his visit, he was Prefect of the Batha Region of Chad. Next to him, in a European style business suit, is Abdoulaye Lamana. His handsome face is marked by tribal patterns of ritual scarification. At the time of his visit to Miami Beach, he was Director of Finance for the Republic of Chad. In later years he spent a number of seasons in political exile in France, returning to Chad in 1986. He left Chad again, this time to serve as Chad's Ambassador to Belgium. Mr. Lamana is currently President of the opposition party, Union Nationale, which he founded in 1992. On the far right, Executive Director of Chad President Tombalbaye's office, Silas Selingar, in a silk suit. The guests spent four days in Miami headquartered at the Shelborne Hotel.

Palm and Eagle
Local and National Characters

Previous spread:
The official seal of the City of Miami Beach, with the date of its incorporation, depicts the land, sea, and sky. Constructs of humankind—a plane, a ship, and a sailboat—inhabit the landscape, but the essential palm icon dominates. To the right of the Miami Beach seal is the emblematic American Eagle.

Opposite:
Backstage at Miami Beach Auditorium, an elderly Eleanor Roosevelt receives a Key to the City of Miami Beach from Mayor Kenneth Oka on October 26, 1961, United Nations Day.

**Mother of
Miami Beach's
25th Mayor**
Mrs. Roosevelt chose The Delano hotel for her stay. The hotel is named for the maternal family of her husband, Franklin Delano Roosevelt. The former First Lady was a United Nation's delegate from its inception in 1945 until 1952. Two years later, her son Elliott arrived in Miami Beach, opened a consulting business, and ended up becoming Miami Beach's 25th Mayor.

**"Choice of
American people
as the woman
they admire most
in the world
today."**
George Gallup, Director, American Institute of Public Opinions, 1958[1]

**The Wolfsons
Go to Washington**
The Wolfsons went to Washington, D.C. in 1952 for the convention of Theatre Owners of America, of which Mr. Wolfson was President. When the Owners' wives toured the White House, Mrs. Wolfson was asked at the last minute to introduce President Truman to the ladies.

According to Maude Massengale's "The Social Sundial" in the Miami Beach *Sun*, she fulfilled her responsibility with great grace and without a slip.[2]

Above:
Frances Wolfson walks down the steps of the White House with President Harry S. Truman. The event was filmed and projected across the screens of America's theaters.

295

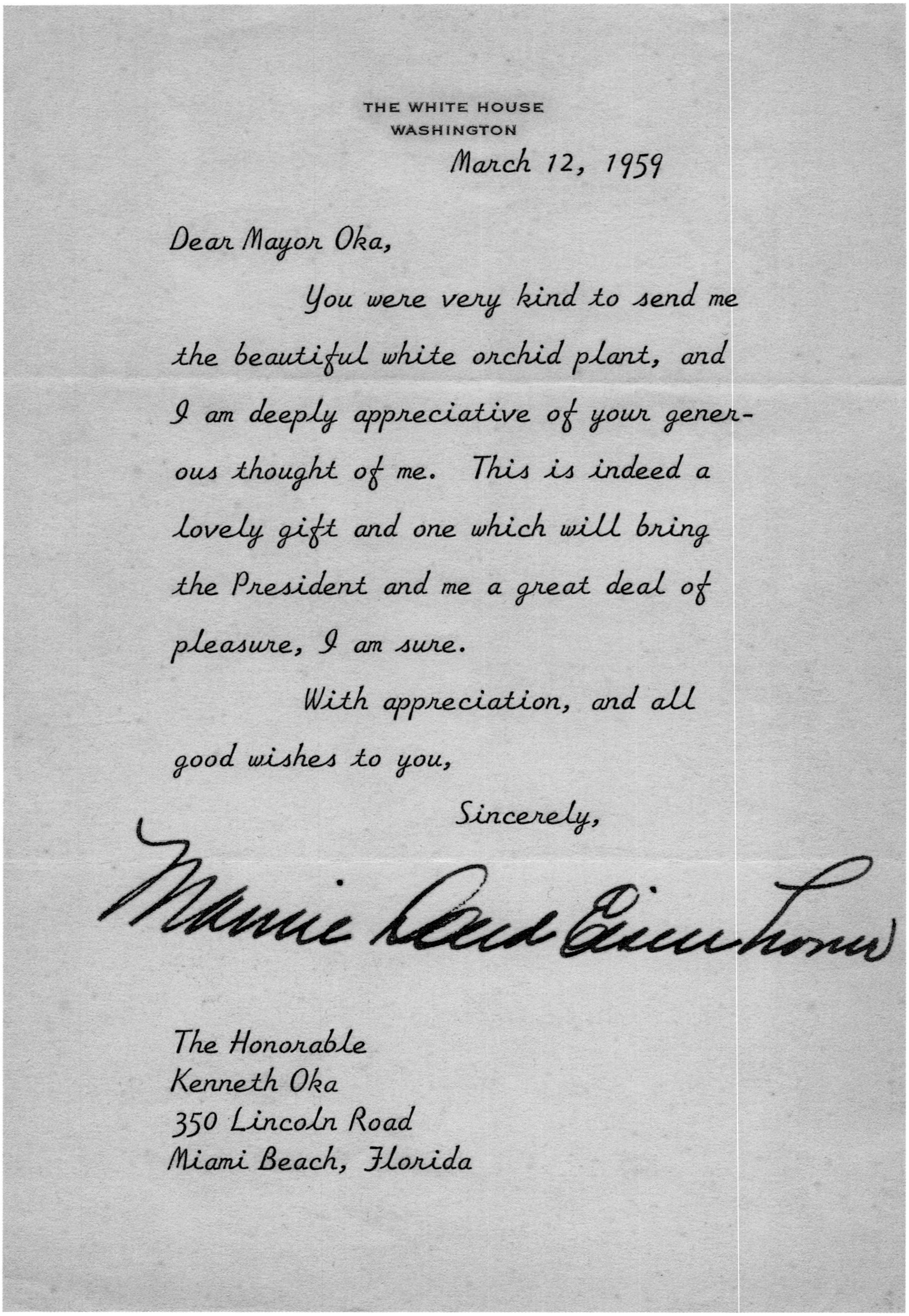

THE WHITE HOUSE
WASHINGTON

March 12, 1959

Dear Mayor Oka,

You were very kind to send me the beautiful white orchid plant, and I am deeply appreciative of your generous thought of me. This is indeed a lovely gift and one which will bring the President and me a great deal of pleasure, I am sure.

With appreciation, and all good wishes to you,

Sincerely,

Mamie Doud Eisenhower

The Honorable
Kenneth Oka
350 Lincoln Road
Miami Beach, Florida

The Eisenhower Era Was "Big Time" for Miami Beach

In 1958, Miami Beach presented its huge Exhibition Hall to the world with Gabriel Heatter, Dean of American News Broadcasting and a resident of Miami Beach for eleven years, telling a listening American audience: **"I'm speaking to you from an exhibition hall three times as large as Madison Square Garden."**[3]

National columnist Sylvia Porter said it all when she quipped, **"They're sleeping in the cabañas."**[4]

Garbage Collection Sets a Record

The "they" included mink-clothed women and Heads of State. Given the number of thank you notes found among Ken Oka's papers, the City of Miami Beach was marketing its image as a tropical paradise with great energy. Garbage collections, the dependable barometer of economic conditions in a resort city, ran at a record high.

Opposite:
American Beauty Roses for the Second Lady
A smiling Pat Nixon ceremonially scissors the ribbon for the National Capital Flower and Garden Show. A garland of embroidered flowers frames her face as the fashionable Vice President's wife does her work. The show drew record crowds of 23,000 people opening day to view two acres of flowers. Mayor Oka was on hand, escorting Japanese Ambassador Koichiro Asakai.[5] Oka holds a bouquet of long-stemmed American Beauty roses to be presented to the Second Lady.

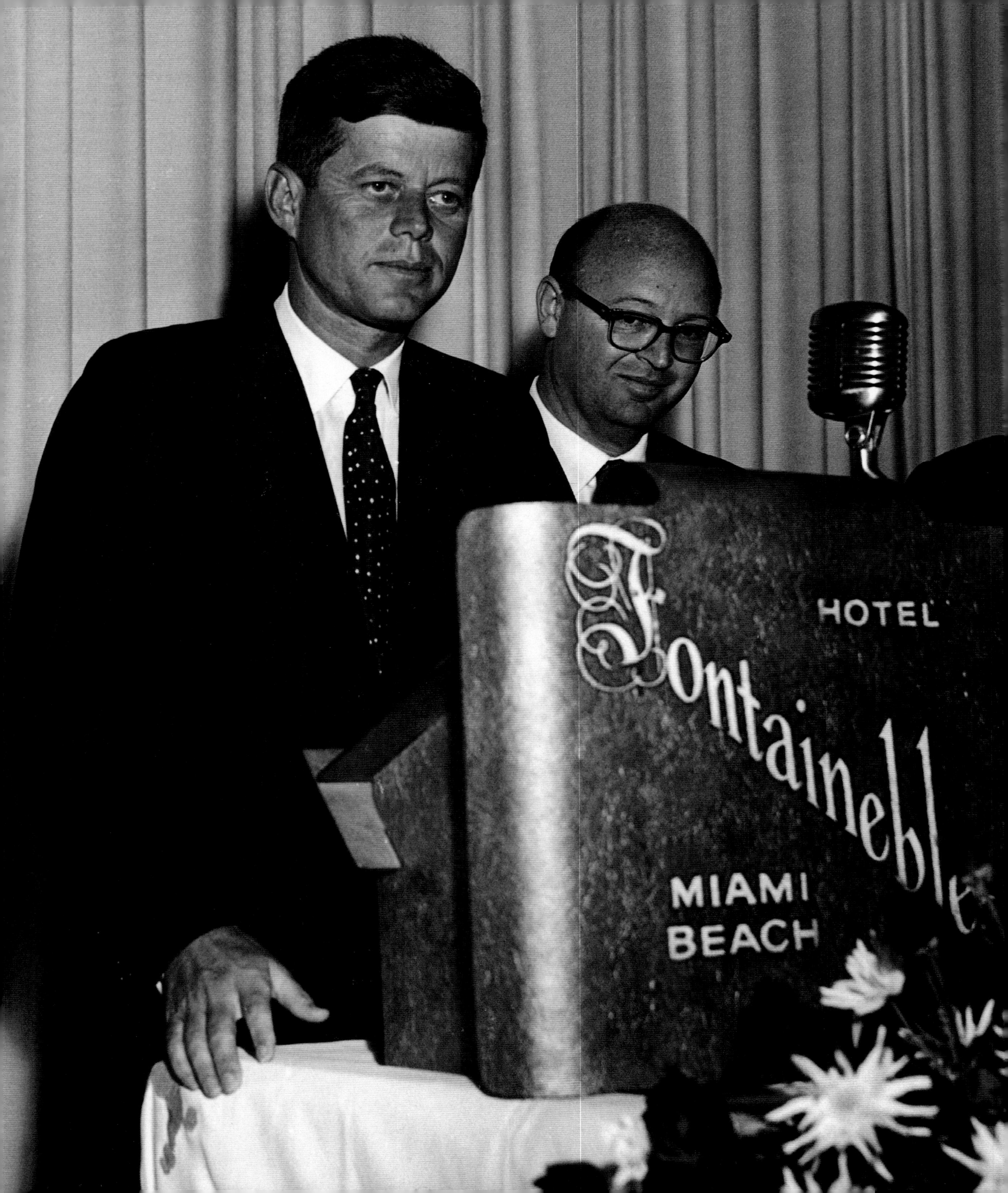
HOTEL
Fontainebleau
MIAMI
BEACH

An Urban Magna Carta

Senator Kennedy was a featured speaker at the 1958 United States Conference of Mayors and addressed a luncheon session of the convention in the Fleur de Lis Room at the Fontainebleau. His speech, "Time for an Urban Magna Carta," urged American mayors to restate, in positive terms, the people's rights demanded of and granted by King John so many centuries earlier in 1215.

Opposite:
Senator John F. Kennedy addressing the United States Conference of Mayors, with Mayor Kenneth Oka paying attention, 1958. Kennedy ended his talk by quoting William Jennings Bryan:
"The humblest citizen of all the land, when clad in the armor of a righteous cause, is stronger than all the hosts of error."

The Ladies Lunched

Gertrude Oka was Official Hostess to the conference. While the men conducted their business, she chaired and charmed a luncheon for more than five hundred wives. In addition to this large affair, Gertrude lunched separately with Jackie Kennedy. When she was interviewed five years later, upon the death of the President, Gertrude recalled that Mrs. Kennedy was apprehensive about her husband serving center stage. She dreaded the loss of privacy that came with the Presidency.[6]

Right:
A pregnant **Jacqueline Kennedy** accompanies her husband.

"[Mrs. Kennedy was a] very honest, forthright person, very humble, unpretentious with a thirst for knowledge and a great respect for people all over the world. She had a feeling for different cultures . . . she felt strongly about family life and giving children a lot of attention although she had only Caroline at the time."
Gertrude Oka

Following spread:
President Kennedy enjoys a Havana and watches the Orange Bowl, New Year's Day, 1963. It was to be his last. Shoulders framing the President are, from left to right, Representative Dante Fascell and Mrs. Farris Bryant (deep in conversation with Frances Wolfson, in profile). Behind her, gazing at the game, is Mitchell Wolfson. Visible behind her is Florida's oldest senator, Claude Pepper. The Secret Service and State Troopers were called in to calm hysterical Alabama cheerleaders who met and shook hands with JFK. That afternoon, Alabama beat Oklahoma 17 to 0.[7]

GARDENS

Eden through the Window, One Step Removed

The diorama behind the plate glass windows of the Exotic Gardens on Lincoln Road is enchanting. The Spanish style building, flanked by two royal palms, featured red-tiled roofs, white stuccoed walls, and rafters of Dade County pine upholding the cathedral ceiling. Specializing in orchids for the body and table, the Exotic Gardens also provided ferns, palms, potted hibiscus for patios, and an assortment of vines that must have evoked ancestral memories of hanging gardens. The Exotic Gardens had their own nurseries, in still rural South Dade County. There they developed the pure white Nellie Donn orchid, a hybrid of the brasso and cattleya varieties.

The Exotic Gardens began its business in the Spring of 1915, the same year that John Collins' Miami Beach Improvement Company offered ocean-front lots at $1,500. James Donn Sr. worked to provide floral arrangements for the wealthy who had plenty of cash to invest in the lots between Biscayne Bay and Indian Creek and build houses and throw parties. Donn arrived in the United States from Scotland expecting to find a land of golden opportunity. After a brief stint in Jacksonville as nursery shrub manager, he moved to Miami and discovered the Gold Coast. His first shop was just south of the Miami River at Fifteenth Road. He built Exotic Gardens from a few tropical plants into one of the world's leading members of FTD, Florists Telegraph Delivery Association.

Still life featuring *Cattleya Trianë*, a large orchid adopted by the early nurseries for its flexibility and superb blossoms. It is one of many foreign species that have become naturalized in South Florida. Up until World War II, there were two dozen varieties of native orchids in most of the hammocks of Dade County. They were striking in their impact, gracefully draped around column-like tree trunks, often from base to top. Several botanists crawled through the dense shrubbery and thorny vines of the Everglades to gain admission to what they termed, "a green-roofed cathedral." For all the mosquitoes and impassable marshy land, they reported it was well worth the trouble.

Excerpts from Kenneth Oka's Speech upon His Retirement from Public Office, 1963

As I sat in my study at home this afternoon, I tried to visualize this evening, to anticipate that friends I would see and the speeches I would hear. What would I say in answer? What could I say?

… Life is exceedingly difficult and frustrating in these days of our years—for people of all ages—more than it has ever been in the world's history. Vietnam—Cuba—the Dominican Republic–China—the threat of the unleashing of nuclear energy. All of it hovers over us like a threatening sword. Life is difficult.

Life is hard for hundreds of millions of people all over the world, and in our own Appalachia, and Georgia and Mississippi—and the slums of America, and believe it or not, in parts of our own Miami Beach.

Solutions have to be found—more quickly today than ever before.

Twenty years of public life have furnished me with a practical encyclopedia of human traits, nature, and behavior. Often during these twenty years I have debated with myself—Is man good or evil, altruistic or selfish?…

… I have never been able to resolve the contradictions… The question becomes—how does one chart his course through life? How does one strive for the good life, for himself and others—near and far?

National Character is formed
at the Local level.

I only can answer from my own experience. I think it is important … for an individual to daily live with a philosophy—a conscious, not an unconscious one. Life is full—it could be beautiful and exciting, and we should, each of us, try to extract from each day something that is worthwhile—something that will make that day richer and more meaningful for us. A new friendship, a new accomplishment, a help to someone distressed, cheer to someone who needs to badly, a new awareness of the physical beauty around us which so many take for granted.

When were you last in bed at night and listen with enjoyment to the whoosh of the tropical wind and rain, or hear the early morning warbling of the bird outside the window?

To those business and medical men who work on Lincoln Road I ask, when, if ever, did you walk the mall in the cool of morning before entering your office for the day, and watch the sparrows bathe in the pool or enjoy the beautiful planting?

Has anyone here ever walked the beach—on the sand, on a Sunday afternoon? …

"Realize that the world is a thrill with beauty and excitement. Keep yourself sensitized to it. Never let yourself get dull. Never lose your enthusiasm. Enthusiasm cannot live in a mind filled with dull, unhealthy and destructive ideas."
Ramesh Pai

… Miami Beach: it is a wonderful city, richly endowed by nature and God. It carries with it the hopes and aspirations of over 75,000 souls, all struggling to find themselves, and to lead the good life.

"National character is formed and nurtured at the local level."
Kenneth Oka

This thought was pencilled in by newly-elected Mayor Oka on his United States Conference of Mayors program when he attended the annual conference at The Waldorf Astoria, New York City, September 9-11, 1957.

A sprig of weeping fig
(Ficus benjamina)

Michele,

Columbus miscalculated. He discovered us instead of India.

He sensed and believed that there was "something out there."
Though he missed the point, geographically speaking, his
mission resulted in a discovery of far greater consequence
than merely landing on an unknown shore. In our case--if we
dare to extend the metaphor--discovery of one thing also led
to another. What we discovered was our particular
relationship to a widely accepted legend. The surprise of
this discovery led us to look for documentation. There it
was--right under our noses.

Reconstructed from all these clues, our story gives substance
to imagination. Personal history, like a novel, is entirely
dependent on its authors.

There's relevance here, not only for those newly arrived on
the scene who recognize what we've uncovered, but for social
historians of the future. Our subject has been the generation
we know best. This glimpse of personal history can become
part of the fabulous panorama of local history.

Micky

Contributors

A Great Lens on the Past
A young **Arnold Newman**, age sixteen or seventeen, still a student at Miami Beach High School. Newman fingers a very sculptural coconut palm tree, c. 1934-35. He now holds an honorary degree, Doctorate of Fine Arts, from the University of Miami.

Previous page:
Pioneer Florist
James Donn Sr., founder of Exotic Gardens on Lincoln Road

Beautiful Trees, Flowers and Some Cheesecake

Hans Hannau was born in Vienna in 1904. As a lawyer in the 1930s, he prosecuted members of Hitler Youth and the SS in Austria, where the Nazi party was banned. During the Nazi occupation of Austria, Hannau was interred in a concentration camp at Buchenwald for six months. Upon his release on February 20, 1939, through a brief amnesty occasioned by Hitler's birthday, Hannau made his way to the United States, arriving in 1940. Because English presented an obstacle to the German-speaking lawyer, he turned to the language of the eye, expressing himself through the camera. Photography had previously been an avocation, but Hannau discovered his talents were marketable. He had a solo exhibit of his photographs at the Gallery Saint Etienne in New York. His cheese-cake postcards of bathing beauties frolicking by the surf were appreciated by large audiences, especially the troops stationed in Miami Beach during World War II. The countless thousands of cards sent up north were probably responsible for the great migration to Miami Beach in post-war years. His first book, *Florida: A Photographic Journey*, was published eight years later and a great success. Hannau went on to publish many books on tropical flowers, gardens, and Caribbean islands. He died in Miami Beach, 2001.

Hannau is pictured here, next to the Cromwell Hotel (page 109), his turf in Eden.

Photo credits:
Hibiscus, 60-61;
Shore Club, 108;
Cromwell Hotel, 109;
Louis and Smitty at Shore Club, 110;
Shelborne Hotel, 113;
Fontainebleau Hotel (postcard), 114-115;
Mana-Zucca, 168;
Palms, 246-247.

Bathing Beauties
Laurence Victor with bathing beauties during the Miss Miami Beach Contest at the Delano Hotel, 1952.

Photo credits:
Kenneth and Gertrude Oka with Rocky Marciano, 258;
Bob Hope, Anita Ekberg, Kenneth Oka at the Eden Roc Hotel, 260, 261.

Too Hot to Handle
Photographer Allen Malschick, on the right, with two of his favorite subjects, Jane Mansfield (40" 18" 36") and Mickey Hargitay, her second husband. Malschick scouted Miami Beach's cabana clubs for action during the heyday years of Wometco's world premiers. Mansfield was a star of *Too Hot to Handle* and *The Girl Can't Help It*. *Variety* magazine said that Mansfield always looked as though she was leaning out of a window.

"She'll never drown."
Comedian Alan King

Photo credits:
Roney Plaza, 102-103;
Zorita and Her Snake, 184-185;
Kenneth Oka and Janet Leigh, 243, 264;
Polly Bergen in Cocktail Dress, 262;
Sammy Walsh, Jill St. John, Kenneth Oka, Robert Evans at Carib Theatre, 265

Ted Press
With one of his favorite subjects, Jackie Gleason. At seventy, Ted Press was still working full time taking pictures for the Miami Beach *Sun*. He worked for the *Sun* for twenty-one years, capturing the great era of the fifties and early sixties as Miami Beach became a magnet and drew the world of glamour and fun to its shores.

Photo credits:
Gertrude Oka at Coronation Ball for Miss Universe, 147; Eleanor Roosevelt, 294; JFK at Orange Bowl Game, 300-301.

Up a Palm Tree
The Navy sent **Chris Hansen** from New Jersey to Miami in 1944. When the war was over, Hansen returned and began work as a photographer, first at the Miami *Herald* and then at The City of Miami Beach News Bureau for twenty-five years.

Photo credits:
Miss Universe on the Beach, 111; Hostess Luncheon for Miss Universe, 286-287; John F. Kennedy, 298; Jackie Kennedy, 299.

Photo Goddess
Born in Teheran, Iran, **Iran Issa-Khan** was raised in Europe and the United States. Her photographs of major figures, from supermodels to royalty, have appeared in *Harper's Bazaar*, *Vogue*, *Elle* and numerous other publications globally. Her current work focuses on the sensuality of tropical plants and seashells. She has exhibited at Staley Wise Gallery in New York, Holly Hunt in Miami, and the Mission Gallery in London.

Photo credits:
Palm seeds, 10-11; Brain coral, 22-23; Oolitic limestone, 80-81; Written in sand by Michele Oka Doner, 270-271.

**Fruiting
and Flowering**
Dr. Julia Morton, botanist, had an encyclopedic knowledge of plant life and a passion for life as well. During the Depression she decided that what the world needed was food. Out of optimism and a sense of purpose, the Morton Collectanea was born and has provided information about food crops for over fifty years. Of the palm, she remarks, **"Look at it. It's beautiful. It's perfect."**

"I knew the Beach Theater could have been anywhere; The Carib was just for Miami."
Michael J. DeAngelis

Creator of The Carib Theatre
Michael J. DeAngelis, architect of many theatres, including The Carib which he described as "the last movie palace in the country." He not only designed The Carib, but named it as well. He understood that all life is theater and this was but another stage set within a stage set.

Next spread, left: Some of the many wonderful theatres that were designed by Michael J. De Angelis for Paramount Theatre Corporation.

Next spread, right: Note from Michael J. De Angelis, architect of the Carib Theater, to Mitchell Wolfson Jr., January 11, 1995.

Postscript
Michael DeAngelis passed away in 1997, but he left us the plans.

OFFICES OF **MICHAEL J. DeANGELIS** F.A.R.A. - N.C.A.R.B.
CERTIFIED BY
- NATIONAL COUNCIL OF ARCHITECTURAL - REGISTRATION BOARDS -
Architects
HIRAM SIBLEY BUILDING, SUITE 409
311 ALEXANDER STREET, ROCHESTER, NY 14604
716-325-3355

JAN. 11/95

MICKY!

Why don't you
Re-Built the
"CARIB" THEATER

I'am Ready

Mike

NEW YORK ATLANTA, GA ROME
BRANCH OFFICE: 618-624 CARNEGIE BUILDING, ATLANTA, GEORGIA 30303

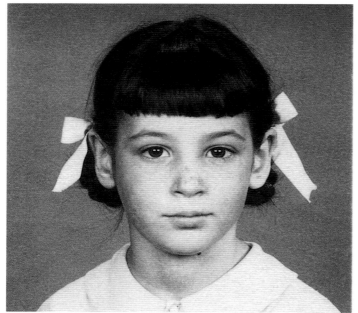

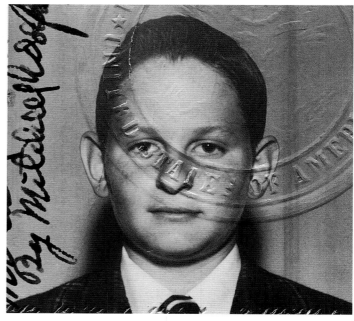

Michele Oka Doner

Mitchell Wolfson Jr.

Born and raised in Miami Beach, Florida, Michele Oka Doner is an internationally acclaimed artist whose prolific career spans four decades. The remarkable breadth of her artistic production encompasses public art, sculpture, furniture, jewelry, and functional objects. She is perhaps best known for her numerous public art commissions, including those at New York's Herald Square Subway Station and the Miami International Airport. Whether for large-scale architectural projects or intimately scaled objects, Oka Doner's work is fueled by a lifelong study and appreciation of the natural world, from which she derives her unique vocabulary. Michele is represented by Marlborough Gallery, New York. Books about her work include *Michele Oka Doner: Natural Seduction*, Hudson Hills Press (2003) and *Michele Oka Doner: Workbook*, OKA Press (2004). Reviews and features on her work have appeared in the New York *Times*, the Washington *Post*, the Miami *Herald*, *ArtNews*, *Sculpture Magazine*, and many other publications in the U.S. and internationally. Oka Doner maintains studios in New York and Miami Beach.

"Micky" Wolfson Jr. was born in Miami, Florida, on September 30, 1939, and was educated at the Lawrenceville School, Princeton University, and the Johns Hopkins School for Advanced International Affairs in Washington, D.C., and Bologna, Italy. Throughout his professional life in America and Italy, he has been an avid accumulator of predominantly American, European, and Japanese decorative and propaganda arts from the period 1885 to 1945. A preservationist rather than a collector in the traditional sense, his museum, the Wolfsonian, founded in 1986, pursues a local educational goal, and encourages international scholarly research in the artistic, social, political, and technological fields of the period and stages acclaimed exhibitions. The museum and its holdings of more than 100,000 items of decorative and fine arts, posters, graphics, archival material, illustrated books, and original documents was donated in 1997 to Florida International University, thereby ensuring the collection's future as an invaluable national asset for present and future scholarship.

"We are more responsible for what we bestow than for what we inherit, and what we do defines us for others and for ourselves."
Mitchell Wolfson Jr.

Bibliography

Agricultural Extension Service. *Native and Exotic Palms of Florida*. Gainesville: University of Florida, 1969.

Barbour, Thomas, *That Vanishing Eden: A Naturalist's Florida*. Boston: Little, Brown and Company, 1944.

Bartram, William, *Travels Through North and South Carolina, Georgia, East and West Florida, etc*. Philadelphia: James & Johnson, 1791.

Brayfield, Lelia and William, *A Guide for Identifying Fossil Shells and Corals*. Pt. Charlotte: William and Lelia Brayfield, 1986.

Bryan, O.C. *Soils of Florida and their Crops Adaptation*. Tallahassee: Department of Agriculture, Bulletin No. 42, June 1960.

Capitman, Barbara Baer, *Deco Delights: Preserving the Beauty and Joy of Miami Beach Architecture*. New York: E.P. Dutton, 1988.

Carson, Rub Leach, *Fabulous Florida: Florida's Story for Children*. Dallas: Manfred, Van North & Co., 1942.

Clearwater, Bonnie. *Frances Wolfson*. The Mitchell Wolfson Family Foundation, 1992.

Collier County Pubic Schools. *Prop Roots Vol. 1 Recipes from the Mangrove Country of The Everglades*. Everglades City: Collier County Public Schools, 1980.

Cooke, C. Wythe. State of Florida Department of Conservation. *Scenery of Florida: Interpreted by a Geologist*. Tallahassee: State Geological Survey, 1939.

Cross, Milton and David Ewen. *Milton Cross Encyclopedia of the Great Composers and their Music*. Volume II. New York: Doubleday & Co., Inc., 1962.

Culot, Maurice and Jean-Francois Lejeune (editors). *Miami: Architecture of the Tropics*. Miami: Center of Fine Arts and Brussels: Archives d'Architecture Moderne, 1952.

Department of Agriculture, State of Florida, Nathan Mayo Commissioner. *Citrus Growing in Florida*. Bulletin No. 2, New Series, November 1931.

Department of Game and Fresh Water Fish. *Florida Birds: Biographies of Selected Species of Birds and Compiled List of All Species Occurring in Florida*. Quarterly Bulletin of the Department of Agriculture, July 1931.

Dorn, Mabel. *Under the Coconut in Florida*. South Miami: The South Florida Publishing Company, 1949.

Federal Writers' Project. *Florida Seafood Cookery*. Bulletin No. 119, Tallahassee: State of Florida Department of Agriculture, Nathan Mayo, Commissioner, June 1943.

Garden Section of the Woman's Club of Havana. *Flowering Plants from Cuban Gardens*. Havana: The Woman's Club of Havana, 1952.

Gifford, John C. *Ten Trustworthy Tropical Trees*. Emmaus, Pa.: Rodale Press, 1946.

Hannau, Hans W. and Jeanne Gerrard. *Tropical Flowers of Florida*. Miami: Argos Inc., n.d.

Hoffmeister, John Edward. *Land from the Sea: The Geologic Story of South Florida*. Coral Gables: University of Miami Press, 1974.

La Gorce, John Oliver. *Treasure-House of the Gulf Stream: The Completion and Opening of the New Aquarium and Biological Laboratory at Miami, Florida*. Republished from the National Geographic Magazine, 1921.

McPhee, John. *Oranges*. New York: Farrar, Straus and Giroux, 1967.

Menninger, Edwin A. *What flowering Tree is That?: A Handbook for the Tropics*. Stuart Florida: Edwin A. Menninger, January 1, 1956.

Menninger, Edwin A. *Seaside Plants of the World*. New York: Hearthside Press, Inc, 1964

Menninger, Edwin A. *Fantastic Trees*. New York: The Viking Press, 1967.

Metro Dade County Office of Community and Economic Development, Historical Preservation Division. *From Wilderness to Metropolis: the History and Architecture of Dade County, Florida 1825 – 1940*. Miami: Metro Dade County, 1982.

Milbank, Caroline Reynolds. *New York Fashion: The Evolution of American Style*. New York: Harry N. Abrams, Inc., 1989.

Morton, Julia F. *500 Plants of South Florida*. Miami: Fairchild Tropical Garden, 1981.

Nash, Charles Edgar. *The Magic of Miami Beach*. Philadelphia: David McKay Company, 1938.

Nehrling, Henry. *The Plant World of Florida*. New York: The MacMillan Company, 1933.

Patricios, Nicholas N. *Building Marvelous Miami*. University Press of Florida, 1994.

Peters, Thelma. *Miami, 1909*. Miami: Banyan Books, Inc., 1984.

Petuch, Edward J. *The Edge of the Fossil Sea: Life Along the Shores of Prehistoric Florida*. Sanibel Island: Bailey-Matthews Shell Museum, 1992.

Rader, Vivian Laramore. *Poinciana Poems*. Miami: Pandanus Press, 1953.

Rare Fruit Council. *Tropical Fruit Recipes: Rare and Exotic Fruits*. Miami: Rare Fruit Council International, Inc., 1981.

Safford, W.E. "Natural History of Paradise Key and the Nearby Everglades of Florida" *Annual Report of the Board of Regents of The Smithsonian Institution*, 1917.

Seeman, Berthold. *Popular History of the Palms and their Allies*. London: Lovell Reeve, 1856.

Simpson, Charles Torrey. *In Lower Florida Wilds: A Naturalist's Observations on the Life, Physical Geography, and Geology of the more Tropical Part of the State*. New York: G.P. Putnam Sons, 1920.

Smiley, Nixon. *Subtropical Gardening in Florida*. Miami: University of Miami Press, 1951.

Snyder, Ethel, *Florida Trees*. Sanibel: Ethel Snyder, 1952.

Sprunt, Jr., Alexander, *Florida Bird Life*. New York: Coward-McCann, Inc. and the National Audubon Society, 1954.

Stearms, Frank F. *Along Greater Miami's Sun-Sea-Ara*. Miami: The City Planning Board, February 1932. Ch 1, p. 8.

Stevenson, George B. *Palms of South Florida*. George B. Stevenson, 1974.

Tomlinson, P.B. *The Biology of Tress Native to Tropical Florida*. Allston, Massachusetts: Harvard University Printing Office, 1980.

Trachtenberg, Stanley (editor), *Dictionary of Literary Biography*. Detroit: Bruccoli, Clark, 1982.

United States Department of Agriculture. "Pineapple Culture in Florida." *Farmers Bulletin* 1237, Washington D.C., November 1921.

Watkins, John V. *Your Guide to Florida Landscape Plants*. Gainesville: University of Florida Press, 1961.

Watkins, John V. and Herbert S. Wolfe. *Your Florida Garden*. Gainesville: University Presses of Florida, 1968.

Weber, Bruce. *Arnold Newman in Florida*. Norton Gallery: David R. Godine, 1987.

West, Erdmann and Lillian E. Arnold. *The Native Trees of Florida*. Gainesville: University Presses of Florida, 1968.

White, William C. Illustrations by Bernard and Harriet Perchik. *Flowering Trees of the Caribbean*, New York: Reinhart & Company, Inc., 1951.

Williams, Winston. *Florida's Fabulous Trees*, World-Wide Publications, 1986.

Writer's Program of the WPA of the State of Florida. *Miami and Dade County Including Miami Beach and Coral Gables*, 1941.

Zieman, Irving, *Miami Beach in Rhyme*. Boston: Meador Publishing Company, 1954.

Florida Audubon Society. *The Florida Naturalist*, Volume 51, No. 1, February 1978.

End Notes

Eden in View: Site and Materials

1. Berthold Seeman, *Popular History of the Palms and their Allies*, London: Lovell Reeve, 1856, p. 4.

2. W.E. Safford, "Natural History of Paradise Key and the Nearby Everglades of Florida," Annual Report of the Board of Regents of The Smithsonian Institution, 1917, p. 434.

3. O.C. Bryan, "Soils of Florida and their Crop Adaptation," Tallahassee: Department of Agriculture, Bulletin No. 42, June 1960.

4. The La Gorce district of Miami Beach, with its famous golf course, takes its name from John Oliver La Gorce. An associate editor of *National Geographic* magazine, he became secretary and treasurer of the short-lived Miami Beach Aquarium located at the terminus of the new MacArthur Causeway on the ocean side of Miami Beach. The aquarium became a resource for studying tropical fish, rapidly building up a world class library with an international collection of valuable volumes. In addition to the library, the structure had numerous tanks supplied with constantly changing seawater and a collection cruiser provided with wells for transporting living marine animals. The aquarium grounds were developed to exhibit a variety of palm species and subtropical flora. The aquarium was privately operated. The developer James A. Allison offered the entire enterprise gratis to the city of Miami Beach, which refused the offer. The City was too young to take on the enormous expense, so one of the finest institutions of its kind in existence was closed.

5. John Oliver La Gorce, "Treasure-House of the Gulf Stream: The Completion and Opening of the New Aquarium and Biological Laboratory at Miami, Florida," republished from the *National Geographic* magazine, 1921, p. 53.

6. Frank F. Stearms, "Along Greater Miami's Sun-Sea-Ara," Miami: The City Planning Board, February 1932, p. 21. The term Sun-Sea-Ara was originated by Mr. C.W. Chase, Sr., Secretary of the Miami Beach Chamber of Commerce. It applies to the lower east coast of Florida from Palm Beach southward. Frank Stearn's booklet, a first edition, is a register of prominent residents whose fine homes adorn the water frontage of the Greater Miami area.

7. Today, all that is left of the Okeechobean Sea is Lake Okeechobee, which is landlocked and, at 700 square miles, is the country's second largest body of freshwater.

8. Edward J. Petuch, *The Edge of the Fossil Sea: Life Along the Shores of Prehistoric Florida,* Sanibel Island: Bailey-Matthews Shell Museum, 1992.

9. There used to be rapids at the point where the Miami River and what is now NW 12th Avenue intersect. The east coast of the rocky edge of the Everglades is slightly elevated, and rapids occurred where the streams broke through on their journey to Biscayne Bay. This elevation was accentuated with the scouring actions of tides, eroding the limestone substrate, often to a depth of six to ten feet. These falls of the Miami River were dynamited in 1905 in order to create a system of drainage canals between the Everglades and Biscayne Bay. After the destruction, the Miami River merged with the Miami Canal.

10. Winston Williams, *Florida's Fabulous Trees*, World-Wide Productions, 1986, p. 26.

Family Tendrils: People Take Root

1. Department of Game and Fresh Water Fish, "Florida Birds: Biographies of Selected Species of Birds and Compiled List of All Species Occurring in Florida," Quarterly Bulletin of the Department of Agriculture, July 1931, pp. 134-136.

2. John McPhee, *Oranges*, New York: Farrar, Straus and Giroux, 1967.

3. The address was 239 NE 14th Terrace (Bougainvillea Court) and is located now in the vicinity of the Performing Arts Center of the future.

4. Arthur E. Curtis & Associates, *This is Greater Miami: Metropolis of the Tropics*, 1947.

5. Mockingbirds and Orange Blossoms, n.d., india ink and handmade water based colors on silk, 30 x 47 inches. Collection of Florida House, Washington, D.C.

6. Nicholas N. Patricios, *Building Marvelous Miami*, University Press of Florida, 1994, pp. 94-95.

7. Margaret Acer, Society Columnist, "Woman Beside the Man: Mitch Whistles; Life is Good," Miami *News,* Thursday, June 12, 1958.

8. Federal Writers' Project, "Florida Seafood Cookery," Bulletin No. 119, Tallahassee: State of Florida Department of Agriculture, Nathan Mayo, Commissioner, June 1943, p. 30.

9. Charles Torrey Simpson, *Ornamental Gardening in Florida,* Little River, Florida: 1926, p. 211.

10. Henry Nehrling, *The Plant World in Florida*, New York: The Macmillan Company, 1933, p. 206.

11. Irving Zieman, *Miami Beach in Rhyme*, Boston: Meador Publishing Company, 1954, p. 208.

12. The Miami *Herald*, Sunday, March 8, 1987, p. B4.

13. William C. White, *Flowering Trees of the Caribbean*, New York: Rinehart & Company, Inc., p. 69. (Thirty paintings by Bernard and Harriet Pertchik)

14. Interview with Shirley Kaufman, kindergarten teacher at North Beach Elementary for almost two decades beginning in 1953.

15. The photograph of Barbara June was taken in 1945. A half-century later, Michele Oka Doner took the photograph to Newman at his New York studio for his signature. He quipped with his pen, "After half a century, here's my signature!" "Boogie Woogie Broadway" still hangs in Newman's New York City apartment.

Dreams and Designs: Architecture in Eden

1. "Scottish Temple Scene of Wedding," wedding announcement in unknown Miami newspaper.

2. Irving Zieman, *Miami Beach in Rhyme*, Boston: Meador Publishing Company, 1954, p. 169.

3. Schultze and Weaver. After they built the Roney Plaza in Miami Beach, the architectural design firm of Leonard Schultze and S. Fullerton Weaver went on to build the Pierre and the Waldorf-Astoria in New York City. Like the Roney, the Pierre, on Fifth Avenue facing Central Park, is a romantic, towered presence. The Waldorf-Astoria, on Park Avenue in midtown, was the epitome of 1930s chic. This world-famous institution has been home to such notables as President Hoover and the Duke of Windsor. The Wolfsonian-FU in Miami Beach holds the Schultze and Weaver archive.

4. Personal interviews with Hans Hannau, 1994 and 1995.

5. Maurice Culot and Jean-Francois Lejeune, eds., *Miami: Architecture of the Tropics,* Miami: Center of Fine Arts and Brussels: Archives d'Architecture Moderne, 1992, p. 72.

6. "Royalty, Other Dignitaries Mingle with Miamians," Miami *Herald*, Monday, January 17, 1955, p. C1.

Shadows of War

1. "Retirement of Gen. Jacob L. Devers," Remarks of Hon. Henry Cabot Lodge, Jr., of Massachusetts in the Senate of the United States, Wednesday, August 3, 1949.

2. City of Miami Beach, Florida, Memorandum from Tom F. Smith to Miami Beach's Committee in Washington, May 20, 1943.

3. "Iron Gates, Fences Sought for Scrap," Miami *Herald*, October 27, 1942.

4. "Roundup of Iron Fences and Gates Opens," *Daily Tropics*, Tuesday, October 20, 1942, p. 18.

5. "Army Center Needs 100 Volunteers," Miami *Herald*, Sunday, June 6, 1943.

6. Letter to Zenia and Sidney Meyers from Mitchell Wolfson, dated August 17, 1943, after a telephone conversation.

Gilding the Fig Leaf: Style on the Beach
1. Seth Faison, "Madame Chiang Kai-shek, A Power in Husband's China and Abroad, Dies at 105," New York *Times*, Saturday, October 25, 2003, p. A15.

Overtures to Culture
1. "Interview of the Week: Judge Kenneth Oka," *Hemisferio*, March 6, 1955, p. 11.

2. Stanley Trachtenberg, ed., *Dictionary of Literary Biography*, Detroit: Bruccoli, Clark, 1982, pp. 110-117.

3. S. Baker, *Biographical Dictionary*, Nicolas Sloninsky, New York: Schirmer Books, 1992, p. 1863.

4. "Walk, Don't Run," *Newsweek*, April 23, 1962, p. 64.

5. "Symphony Club's Record: $204,579 in Seven Years," Miami *Herald*, April 8, 1959.

6. William G. Moeser, "Strippers at Beach Baring More Than Ever," Miami *News*, undated.

The Showmandisers: Building an Empire
1. "WTVJ Reports Progress during its First Year," Miami *Daily News*, Tuesday, April 11, 1950, p. 17B.

2. "Opening Program Lists Top Flight TV Offerings," Miami *Daily News*, Sunday, March 20, 1949, p. 23C.

3. William S. Paley, "Video Viewed as Boon to Democracy and Free World by Paley of CBS," Miami *Daily News*, Sunday, March 20, 1949, p. 23C.

4. Miami *Herald*, Wednesday, October 25, 1967, p. 11C.

5. Collier County Pubic Schools, Prop Roots Vol. 1, Recipes from the Mangrove Country of The Everglades, Everglades City: Collier County Public Schools, 1980.

6. Department of Agriculture, State of Florida, Nathan Mayo Commissioner, "Citrus Growing in Florida," Bulletin No. 2, New Series, November 1931.

7. Brochure, Clermont, Florida, Citrus Tower Packing House, 1955.

8. *Kim's Guide to Florida,* Fifth Annual and Special Edition for Florida's Exhibition at the 1939 World's Fair, Anna Maria, Florida: Kim's Guide, 1939, p. 19.

9. "Florida Company Entertains Its Owners," *Business Week*, April 22, 1961, pp. 106-107.

Caribbean Eden: Tropical Movie Palace
1. "The Kid Won't Get out of the Picture: Robert Evans is Playing Robert Evans Again," New York *Times*, Sunday, November 2, 2003, p. 14.

The Stars at Night: Hollywood on Miami's Stage Set
1. T. D. Allman, *Miami: City of the Future*, New York: The Atlantic Monthly Press, 1987, p. 250.

2. Program, the Miracle Theatre inaugural performance, December 7, 1948.

3. Robert D. McFadden, "Hoboken to Hollywood and Beyond: Mourning the Man and His Magic," New York *Times*, Saturday, May 16, 1998, p. B18.

4. "Music and Marriage Starred at Wometco: Wolfson, Meyer in Harmony," Miami *News*, Sunday, August 10, 1958, p. 2.

5. David Wallechinsky and Irving Wallace, *The People's Almanac*, Garden City: Doubleday and Co., 1975, p. 1148.

6. *The New Yorker*, July 14, 1997.

7. Caryn James, "Jean Seberg's Life, Most of It True," New York *Times*, October 11, 1995.

8. New York *Times*, Sunday, March 25, 2001.

9. Emphaim Katz, *The Film Encyclopedia*, New York: Harper Perennial, 1994, p. 1194.

10. Program, The Third Annual Hollywood Film Festival, August 4-9, 1999.

11. David Pirie, *Anatomy of the Movies*, New York: Macmillan Publishing Co., Inc., p. 58.

World's Playground: Keys to the City
1. Bob Terrell, "Putting Something into the Soil," Asheville *Citizen*, April 1, 1975.

2. "Look Who Dropped in at the Stork: Mob Was at the Back Door as Stars Lined Up in Front," New York *Times*, Monday, July 1, 1996, pp. B1-2.

Palm and Eagle: Local and National Characters
1. George Gallup, Director, American Institute of Public Opinion, quoted in the program of "The 1st Annual American Resort Fashion Award."

2. Maude Massengale, Miami Beach *Sun*, September 18, 1952.

3. Si Steinhauser, "Beach Presents its Huge Exhibition Hall to the World," Miami Beach *Sun*, Tuesday, October 28, 1958.

4. Sylvia Porter, "They're Sleeping in the Cabanas," Miami *Herald*, Tuesday, March 10, 1959.

5. "Flower Show Attracts Record 23,000 Crowd," Washington *Star,* March 9, 1959.

6. Harry R. Betters, editor, City Problems of 1958, The Annual Proceedings of the United States Conferences of Mayors, Miami Beach, Florida, September 11-14, 1958, Washington: The United States Conference of Mayors, 1958, p. 33-37.

7. Janet Schumir, "The Day Jacqueline Kennedy Wished...", Miami Beach *Daily Sun*, Wednesday, November 27, 1963.

8. "Kennedy Adds Thrill to Orange Bowl Color," Miami Beach *Daily Sun*, Wednesday, January 2, 1963.

9. Charles T. Simpson, *Native and Exotic Plants of Dade County, Florida*, Washington D.C.: Press of Judd & Detweiler, Inc., n.d., p. 45.

Acknowledgements

Miami Beach: Blueprint of an Eden was created with the help of many individuals. Lea Nickless was instrumental in shaping our vision, and served as a liaison to the Wometco archive. Her love and knowledge of bookmaking is visible on these pages. Jordan Schaps, creative guru, gave the book its form. Together, we laid out the initial concepts and prioritized the multitude of materials in our families' archives. The late poet John Malcomb Brinnan was with us in the beginning, offering advice on how to take the personal and particular and open it to new interpretations. Joe Tashiro was generous with his family archive and recollections, allowing us to add to our story the transformative nature of his father's magic. S. Tashiro's early photographs of Miami Beach are the jewels of this book. Barbara Bloemink, Chief Curator of the Cooper-Hewitt National Design Museum in New York, offered many suggestions and much enthusiasm in the early stages. We are grateful to Charlotte Seeling, garden curator, for recognizing Miami Beach as Eden. Interviews with Shirley Kaufman, the kindergarten teacher at North Beach Elementary School, and Soli Moustaki, Miami's own couturier, were full of joy, insight, and wisdom. The late photographer Hans Hannau presented us with a bounty of visual material. Judith Youngerman Gindy, the modern dance teacher, and children's designer Sylvia Whyte were also generous, sharing their creative lives.

We thank the University of Miami Geology department for the photographs of ooids, and the late Julia Morton for her transparencies, time and interest.

Finally, we remember the architect Michael de Angelis for the gift of the Carib Theatre drawings, his memories of the Wolfson Family and Miami Beach in the late 1940s, as well as his irrepressible energy. Our visit with him in Rochester, New York, was a highlight of our experience creating this book.

Photo Credits

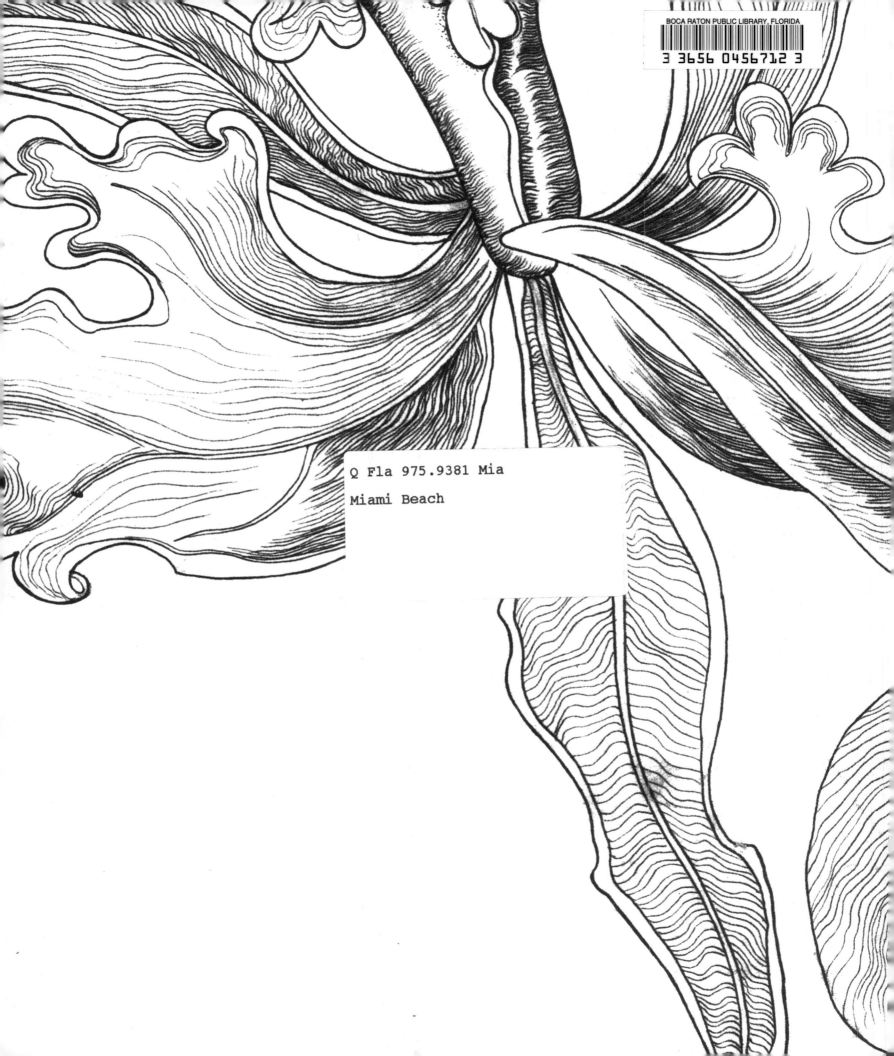